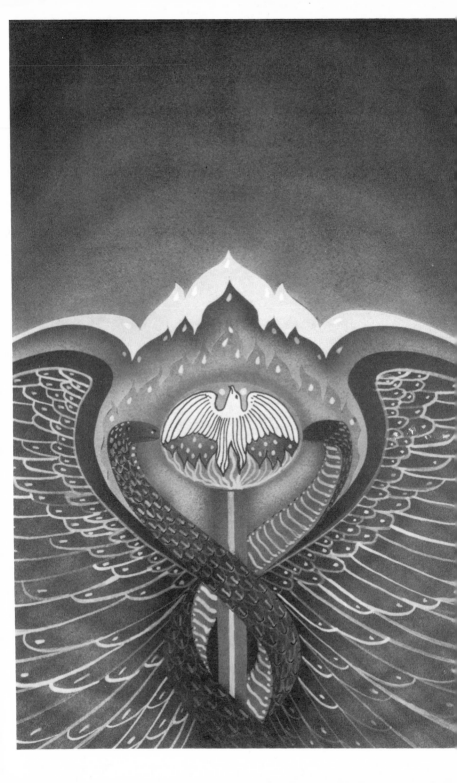

CASENOTES OF A

MEDICAL ASTROLOGER

CASENOTES
OF A
MEDICAL ASTROLOGER

Margaret Millard M.D.

SAMUEL WEISER
NEW YORK

First published in 1980 by
Samuel Weiser, Inc.
740 Broadway
New York, N.Y. 10003

ISBN 0-87728-484-9

Typesetting and layout by
Positive Type
Millerton, N.Y.

Printed in the U.S.A. by
Noble Offset Printers, Inc.
New York, N.Y. 10003

INTRODUCTION

My friend, Margaret Millard, has asked me to write a short introduction to this book, and I am happy to do so.

Astrology today is at something of a crossroads. There are broadly two schools of thought among present day students. On the one hand, a considerable corpus of astrological lore has been handed down from remote times. The present century has seen a revival of this knowledge and a determined effort to put it into some kind of good order, to refine and improve some of the techniques upon which its application must depend, to bring greater psychological insight into the interpretative art, and generally to get more mileage out of the traditional rules.

At the same time, some astrologers have decided that there is so much that is distorted and doubtful in the old rules that it is better to set them aside and start again, taking nothing for granted and trying to rebuild the science step by verifiable step from the beginning.

In the studies contained in this book Dr. Millard has aligned herself primarily with those who are prepared to make full use of traditional knowledge and, while retaining a due measure of scepticism especially in relation to medical topics, to rely largely on the "received" alphabet of astrological judgement.

My own approach, as it happens, is more in accord with the second standpoint which prefers to assume very little, and to favor a fresh stand in reassessing the fundamentals of astrology. Nevertheless I believe that this work has a great deal to offer the student which he will not easily find elsewhere.

In the first place we are given a fine selection of unusual and interesting charts with accurate birth times which will provide valuable material for all students whatever interpretative techniques they may favor. In the second, we have a book on medical astrology written by someone with expert medical knowledge, and this in itself is a rarity. The studies, too, are thoroughly sympathetic and, above all, largely the result of personal observation and firsthand knowledge. Add to this the clear and readable style of the vignettes contained in the case histories, and the student should have every reason to be grateful for this book.

Insofar as the traditional division of the chart into houses can be sustained, I agree with the author that the Topocentric system (which is very close to Placidus at most latitudes) is thoroughly valid and, more important still, that the value she attaches to oblique ascension, as demonstrated in the penultimate chapter, is probably of basic importance. The attention she draws to the significance of parans is also, needless to say, well justified.

Despite my strong belief in the need for radical research and reassessment in astrology, I have never been among those who thought it wise to ignore or reject tradition, and if many of the charts in this book, taken in conjunction with the accompanying case histories, only serve to convince me that we know very little and need to examine anew the basic tenets of our science, yet I have no doubt that studies such as those Dr. Millard has given us have a most useful and necessary place in our literature, and I hope my fellow students will think likewise.

John M. Addey
May 1979

Contents

Preface 1
Medical Astrology Today 2
Principles of Diagnosis 8
Directions 13
Parts of the Body 16
Do Biorhythms Work? 20
A Few Words About Harmonics 24
The Royal Curse 27
A Fateful Eclipse 32
The Finger of God 35
An Old-Fashioned Treatment
        for an Old Affliction 42
An Impossible Diagnosis 47
A Slight Case of Murder? 52
Never Believe a Patient 60
Never Bet a Dollar
        on a Horse Called Eternity 67
The Gorgon's Head 70
An Impeccable Warrior 74
A Lonesome Road 80
A Far, Far Better Way 85
Playing God 91
Like A Butterfly 96
Knowledge is Power 100
The Many Faces of Love 106
A Case of Iatrogenic Disease 110
Hobson's Choice 116
An Unfortunate Pair of Twins 120
A Child with One Brain 124
Jupiter Combust 129
A Case of Leukemia 135
Why Johnnie Could Not Draw 139
The Luck of the Irish 145
Ancient Wisdom 151
The Cosmos, A Computer 153
The Prenatal Epoch 169
Wherever She May Be 177
The Phoenix 182
Glossary 184
Bibliographic References 187

To my daughter Bronwyn, wherever she may be.

Preface

I am an astrologer. Hundreds of years ago, every physician was an astrologer, but now I am one of only a few. I believe that the diseases from which a patient suffers can be predicted as possibilities from the birth chart. "As above, so below," we astrologers say, and the pattern in the Cosmos at the time of an event is directly related to the kind of event it will be.

A patient with a badly placed Venus will not be able to balance the energies of the body. A patient with an overactive Mars will have high fevers and be accident prone. Someone whose Jupiter is unrestrained by other planets is less likely to be able to check the growth of a cancer, which begins as wild proliferation of certain tissues. If Neptune is too powerful, the patient will be overfearful and may bring about the very afflictions which are feared. If Mercury is the disease indicator, there will be a breakdown of the internal communications of the body. If Saturn is strong, the patient will be able to endure a great deal, but may suffer from bone diseases. If the Moon is in aspect to the more difficult planets, the "malefics," there will be danger in infancy, and psychological troubles due to the influence of the mother. If Pluto is in aspect to Venus, intense sexuality will bring many experiences into the life. If the Sun is prominent and well placed, the health will be good and the ego strong.

A look at the birth patterns of my patients has taught me much about their diseases. The case notes which follow show how medical astrology can be used.

Medical Astrology Today

I think that we have to test everything that has been written about medical astrology, because it is all so old and because we have learned so much about disease and the way the body works in this century.

About twenty years ago a professional astrologer gave a lecture to medical students in England and was foolish enough to read a long list of archaic diseases which had been associated with the twelve signs some hundreds of years ago. Unfortunately, the outmoded medical beliefs caused paroxysms of derisive laughter, as one might expect. These old books have been copied over and over again by modern authors, few of whom know much about the diseases of today.

For example, there is an aphorism attributed to Ptolemy which states that one should not operate on the part of the body ruled by the sign holding the Moon at the time of surgery. In the time of Ptolemy, to undergo surgery was to take your life in your hands. Today, very few patients are deemed too sick for an operation, and it is common to see a 70 year old man having his prostate removed, or a 70 year old woman with a broken hip being pinned. One expects all of them to survive.

The only way I could test this aphorism was to take a series of cases in which some of the patients were not expected to live, but the risk of doing nothing outweighed the possible risk of surgery. The only group in which this can be studied is the heart surgery patients. I obtained the records for the date and time of surgery and the results for the first two years of open heart surgery in my hospital. There were approximately

200 cases, which were evenly spread throughout the year, since two cases weekly were scheduled.

The Moon was in each sign sixteen to seventeen times. The mortality was 15%. Some died at the time, some died in the intensive care unit in the first few days after surgery, and others died several weeks later. Of course the mortality rate is not as high now— it has been reduced to about 5% for serious cases.

There was no excess mortality when the Moon was in Leo. All the signs fell close to the average except Pisces, where the score was double the others. It is possible that the two surgeons who did all the cases both had an afflicted Pisces. Unless these results hold true for other institutions and other surgeons, one cannot say that there is any significance in them. However, they do show that the old aphorism is not true.

The diseases which the planets are said to signify should be questioned. Modern authors say quite categorically that the Sun in Leo gives a tendency to heart disease. As one person in three nowadays dies of heart disease, or artery disease, this is certainly not true.

Culpepper, whose *Astrological Judgement of Disease* was recently published by the American Federation of Astrologers, says, "The Sun causes Pimples and Burles in the face, afflictions of the heart, Heart-burning, Tremblings, Faintings, Tympanies, sore Eyes, and diseases of the mouth, Cramps, Convulsions, all diseases of the Heart and Brain, and their attendants, viz the nerves and arteries, stinking breath, Catharrs, rotten Feavers, thus Authors. And if any ask why I mention no more, tell them here's more than is true." So we see how archaic medical astrology is today, and how much needs to be done to clarify the rules.

The body is an extraordinarily efficient self-regulating system, and everything reacts with everything else. I find the physiological effects of the planets in the houses more useful than the so-called 'anatomical rulerships.' Diseases of different anatomical structures can cause identical symptoms, and the chart, which is symbolical, does not show actual reality, but how the native perceives and reacts to it.

The first house is concerned with consciousness. Injuries to the head which cause brain damage, high fevers which cause hallucinations, endocrine disturbances which cause altered mental states, and brain tumors all are first house matters.

Migraine headaches, because the pain is felt in the head, have a Mars-first house connection as part of their signature.

The second house is concerned with homeostasis and keeping the body regulated within a narrow physiological range. It rules our possessions, and in medical astrology, our blood, electrolytes, hormones, and the intake of nutriments are second house matters. The pituitary gland, which controls all the other endocrine organs, is under this axis. The manufacture and intake of the necessary substances to maintain the homeostasis of the body also come under the second house. Diabetes is a well known second house disorder.

The third house has rulership over the lungs. I did not realize until I studied yoga that the lungs were more than mere organs to oxygenate the blood, and that they were intimately connected with the vitality of the body. They may indeed be the key to radiant health, peace of mind, and longevity. Few people know how to make proper use of them.

The function of the lungs is to provide the body with oxygen which is necessary for life, and to increase the vital energy, which is called *Prana* in the East, and according to sacred doctrine may substitute to some extent for food. It is claimed that the *Prana* can be increased in the body by certain breathing exercises. It is also claimed that the brain is nourished by *Prana*, but as to this I cannot say, for the whole matter is very controversial. We in the West are only now beginning to understand some of the teachings of the East.

Mental deficiency is said by Carter to be associated with water afflictions in the third house, either by sign or planet.

The fourth house rules nutrition and the intake of food. It is also connected with the mother, and the psychologists tell us that early childhood experiences of conflict with the mother can give rise to all kinds of oral fixations in later life. Food is associated with security, and over-eating may be the response

to anxiety and stress. Disturbances of nutrition, either obesity
or starvation, come under the fourth house.

The fifth house rules the heart. It is intimately associated
with the function of the eleventh house, which is concerned
with maintaining the circulation. The heart is a muscle, and a
myocardial infarct, in which the blood supply to the muscle is
cut off and the organism dies, is associated with Mars-Uranus-
Sun contacts with the fifth house. Any malefic in the fifth
house, or ruling it, or in hard aspect to its cusp, shows the
likelihood of heart disease. It is said that each house affects the
one following, and certainly over-eating is one of the factors
which predisposes one to heart disease. Another factor is lack
of exercise, which should be one of the outlets for the energy of
Mars. If it is not, Mars may take revenge.

The sixth house, that of Virgo in the natural zodiac, has
always been thought by astrologers to be ruled by Mercury.
The asteroids Vesta and Ceres are now considered by some
researchers to be the true rulers of Virgo and the sixth house.
The sixth house is the house of illness, and also of work. I find
that a stellium of planets or an important planet in the sixth is
associated with disease which has a hereditary basis, either
genetic, or due to birth or pre-birth injury. Classical astrology
holds the fourth house to be associated with hereditary
disease, but I do not agree. Vesta, the goddess of home,
hearth, and ancestors, is the probable ruler of genetic sixth
house afflictions. It is particularly dangerous to have the same
sign on the cusp of the sixth and seventh houses, as a
hereditary disorder is then sure to manifest itself.

The seventh house is often the significator of death. The
brain usually fails first, and the axis of the first and seventh
houses represents brain death.

The eighth house rules the excretion of those substances
which have been metabolised, their essential portions utilized,
and which now must be eliminated. It therefore completes the
balancing function of the second house. Kidney failure, since
the kidneys are one of the main organs of excretion, comes
under the eighth house. The eighth house also rules the colon.
Any disorder which damages the organs responsible for
homeostasis, namely, the hormones of the central nervous

system, the pituitary-adrenal axis and the endocrine glands dependent on it, is under the second-eighth house.

The ninth house is concerned with the highest part of the brain, the cerebral hemispheres, ruled by Jupiter and Neptune, Jupiter ruling the left and Neptune the right hemisphere.

The tenth house rules the body image, and together with the fourth, is associated with metabolism. Either obesity or starvation can result from disturbances in the function of the axis. Saturn and the tenth house are more likely to cause starvation, such as *anorexia nervosa*, and the Moon and the fourth more likely to be associated with obesity.

The eleveth house rules the circulation, which is directly dependent on the function of the heart, but may fail first, as in cases of hemorrhage.

The twelfth house is associated with autoimmune diseases. These are those where the body mistakes its own tissues for foreign substances, and destroys them. A body should have the power to heal. If the twelfth house is afflicted, the body loses its power to recognise its own structures, and destroys them. The twelfth house is where we are most vulnerable, and negative thoughts can cause a breakdown in the resistance of the body. The functions of the thymus, which produces T lymphocytes, neccessary for immunity, and the liver, which manufactures certain proteins used in the synthesis of the many gamma globulins, which are also neccessary for immunity, are associated with the twelfth house and its rulers Neptune and Jupiter. Neptune is the main planet of serious diseases such as cancer, and the 6-12 axis is that of health and illness.

The ruler of a house is the main indicator for matters represented by the house, and the planets in it play only a secondary part. Even if the sixth house contains malefics, the native will be healthy if the ruler is well placed and free from affliction. If the ruler is afflicted, the disease which will manifest itself will be shown by the house of the ruler, or by the planet which disposes of it.

It is not propitious for health to have the ruler of the sixth or twelfth houses in the sixth or twelfth, because the body will have poor powers of self-healing. Neptune can be particularly deadly.

The signs have a sympathy with the houses. For example, Mars in Gemini, even if it is not in the third house natally, may signify inflammatory lung disease.

There has been little medico-astrological research of value. The scheme I have worked out has been developed empirically over the years by the study of many cases, for I have always studied the charts of my patients instead of relying on the books. The little that has been published is mostly disproving of tradition, as, for example, the first Vernon Clark experiment carried out eighteen years ago, in which I was asked to take part. The task was to find out which of a pair of charts belonged to a child with severe cerebral palsy. A dozen astrologers were given ten pairs of charts. None of the traditional rules seemed to hold true, and none of us did very well, although the results were better than chance. One of the most convincing findings, however, when the results were in, was the affliction of the third house, usually by Neptune.

Charles Carter published an interesting study in *The Astrology of Accident*, in which he stated quite definitely that Aries seemed not to be unduly prominent in accidents to the head, but that the first house was always afflicted. This agrees with my own findings and those of Donald Bradley, who reported that Aries positions were actually lower than would be expected by chance when head injuries were studied.

Principles Of Diagnosis

Medical diagnosis from a chart is difficult. One must look at the pattern, particularly noticing if the Ascendant or sixth cusp or their rulers are part of the main configuration. A pattern which is dominated by a *T* square, *Y* formation or Grand Cross will show problems to be worked out which may relate to health.

The most powerful configuration is the grouping of three planets in such a way that two are in sextile and both in 150 degree aspect to the third. This is known as *Yod* or *Y* formation, and as it has a nature related to the sixth and eighth houses influences the health. The sesquiquadrate or 135 degree aspect is also important. It may be that a planet on the West side of the chart is 135 degrees from the Ascendant, and to find the Moon there is common in infant mortality cases. The Moon, especially when waning, can be malefic.

The eighth house shows more life-threatening illnesses than the sixth, as it is concerned with experiences which bring us out of our daily concerns, such as bringing us close to death. The sixth shows diseases which are hereditarily determined or present from birth.

An eclipse on the twelfth or sixth cusps often ushers in a time when considerations of health are prominent. An eclipse in aspect to the eighth cusp, including the 22.5 degree aspect, may herald death. Eclipses are our best timing device in medical astrology. South Node eclipses are particularly evil.

Cardinal signs are associated with acute conditions, myocardial infarcts (since the heart is a muscle, and Mars, ruler of Aries, the first of the four cardinal signs, is the general ruler of muscles), as well as infections, operations, and accidents. Mars combined with Uranus often signifies sudden death from a myocardial infarct. The Sun is also often involved in these cases.

Fixed signs are associated with long lasting chronic diseases such as arthritis, malignant disease, and metabolic diseases, for example, diabetes. These are usually incurable.

Mutable signs are associated with disturbances of the autonomic nervous system such as migraine, a 6th-9th house affliction. Autonomic nervous diseases comprise most of those for which modern medicine has no cure, such as asthma, spastic colitis, hypertension, peptic ulcers, headaches, and certain kinds of backaches, tendinitis and other painful disorders which some psychologists today think are due to energy blocks. They can be treated by biofeedback or acupuncture better than by drugs, and seem to be caused by the mind rather than a breakdown of body systems.

It must be remembered that diseases only appear in certain environments, and even if the signature for the disease is present, it will not appear unless the environment permits it. The mode of action of a planet is shown by the sign in which it is placed, but the field in which it will operate is shown by the house. A planet in its own sign is strong for good or evil, and a retrograde planet is also strong, since it is then closest to the Earth; but the action appears rather more inward than outwardly apparent.

It is difficult to distinguish between the chart of someone who is a victim of violence and that of the person who committed the violent action. So it is with disease. A doctor who specializes in a disease is likely to fall victim to it, and this has always been understood in the medical profession. My old chief, a urologist, used to pray nightly, "Oh, Lord, when Thou takest me, take me not through the bladder." Cancer specialists are particularly apt to die of cancer and psychiatrists to commit suicide.

Dennis Elwell, an English astrologer for whom I have great admiration, believes that the way to deal with energies is to go along with them. "The antidote for a strong Mars influence in the chart," he says, "is to engage in some vigorous Martial exercise—not to stifle the energy by cultivating the virtues of the opposite planet." This is good advice for a medical astrologer. One must tap into the energies, but divert them to a different level, or, as Dennis Elwell says, "go upstream to the Source."

The sign and house position of the Sun are probably only of value in determining the vitality of the native, and have little or nothing to do with the type of disease. People seem to be divided into those who resemble their Ascendent, those who resemble their Sun, and those who resemble their Moon. Degree influences are very important, but there is no consenus of opinion on them. I carried out a survey of 200 patients whom I was treating for obesity, found no predominance in any of the Sun signs, and so it goes with most of the few other studies that have been made.

It is probable that every disease has a 'signature' of planets involved, but few are known. Diabetes is shown by Venus-Pluto-Jupiter contacts involving the 2-8 axis. Congenital heart disease is a Saturn-Venus affliction. Polio is a Pluto-Mercury disease. Pluto has to do with deep-seated and incurable conditions, and is nearly always prominent in cases of malignant disease. The signature for hemophilia has been beautifully elucidated by Charles Harvey in a classical study published in *Astrology Now* Vol. 1, No. 7, Oct. 1975. He studied the descendants of Queen Victoria, and he found that her Saturn at 28 46' Pisces and her Mars-Saturn midpoint at 8 10' Aries were repeated in the charts of those of her descendants who had hemophilia. Not only these exact points, but also the positions 45 degrees in aspect from them were duplicated, and only in one case out of 24 were the orbs greater than one degree.

It would be interesting to study other hemophiliac pedigrees to see if these same points were important.

The following guide to diagnosis should not be taken literally. Astrological symbolism can be expressed in many ways.

For example, Dennis Elwell, who is one of England's best astrologers, studied a group of children with Downs syndrome. He used equal houses and found a 'sympathy' between the Sun and Saturn, i.e. a connection in some way between the principles involved. He also found a connection between Mars and Mercury, and the 12th house. Mercury was often retrograde. The connection may not be obvious. Mars may be in a sign of Mercury, or Mercury in a sign of Mars. Mercury may have a square of opposition to Mars, or it may be in septile or octile aspect, meaning that it may be 51 degrees 26 minutes away, the septile, or 22 degrees 30 minutes away. These are valid aspects.

Mercury and Mars may be in the same parallel of declination. Close parallels have a very physical effect.

The twelfth house ruler may be at the midpoint of Mars and Mercury.

There may be a mundane square at that latitude. Cyril Fagan first drew the attention of the astrological world to these, and Robert Hand has elaborated the theme further, applying it to transits.

For example, in the latitude of 43 North, when Algol in 25 Taurus is on the 4th cusp, the first degree of Aquarius is rising. These points are in mundane square, because they will come to angles simultaneously. This aspect is known as a 'paran'. The stations of the planets during the year are also sensitive points. If Mars turns from direct to retrograde motion, or from retrograde to direct, which it will do once or twice every year, this degree is a sensitive point with the influence of Mars until his next station. This rule also applies to the stations of planets *before* birth, as long as the child is in the uterus. A child born with Mercury conjunct the previous station of Mars will then be under a Mars-Mercury influence, which will operate in the house ruled by Mercury.

Although I believe that the position of the house ruler is more important than the planet which occupies a house, it is certain that a house is weakened by having a malefic occupy it, especially if there are no good supporting aspects to the malefic. It will manifest itself as trouble of some kind, either a lesson to be learned or something to overcome, and as many lessons are taught by disease, this may be one of the ways in which it will act. There are certain houses which act together, and these are linked by square aspect. So, for example, planets in the fifth and eighth will give sexual problems, either sterility, venereal disease, diseases of the male or female sex organs, frequent miscarriages, or something in some way connected with the function of reproduction. Planets in the fifth and second are likely to show heart disorders connected with electrolyte imbalance, salt retention and so forth. Planets in the second and eleventh may point to endocrine imbalance or failure of homeostasis leading to circulatory problems. Nothing can be considered in isolation.

If the 6th house ruler is involved in any of these planetary pictures, disease is almost certain.

The fixed stars may be very important, but the old rules are not reliable, and a great deal of research must be done before we can use them properly.

Directions

I use primary, secondary, and tertiary directions in my work. Primary directions are based on the rotation of the Earth. In one day, from one noon to the next, the Earth rotates through 360 degrees 59 minutes 8 seconds of arc, and the measure in primary directions equates 0 degrees 59 minutes 8 seconds to a year. They are difficult to calculate, but worthwhile because they act within a week, at most two weeks, when they do act.

Secondary directions are the usual 'day for a year' measure, and they are used by almost all astrologers. In practice there is considerable confusion about the way they should be calculated. There are several methods, each of which gives a different Ascendant for a given date and time.

Chester Kemp has pointed out that the true method should be based on the time taken by the Sun to move through 360 degrees. Nearly everyone thinks of a year in terms of 365 days, or 366 days in a leap year. The method of Chester Kemp is more accurate, and I always use it.

It works as follows. Referring to Chapter 12: *A Slight Case of Murder*, we will compute the secondaries for 7 p.m. E.S.T. March 18, 1977, using the chart of the wife, born at 3 p.m. on May 13, 1915, in Portland Maine.

Transiting Sun	28 Pisces 16 or 328 16'
Natal Sun	22 Taurus 24 or 52 24'
Difference	275 52'

So if the Sun moves through 360 degrees in 24 hours, it moves through 275° 52' in 24 X 275.866/360 or 18 hours 23 minutes.

We therefore add 18 hours 23 minutes to the time of birth, plus 61 days for 61 years.

Time of birth: 3 p.m. E.S.T. May 13, 1915 plus 61 days 18 hours 23 minutes equates to 9.23 a.m. E.S.T. on July 14, 1915.

Tertiary directions are not used by many American astrologers. They were discovered by Troinsky and are extensively used in Europe. They are based on the rule ONE TROPICAL MOON MONTH AFTER BIRTH EQUALS ONE SUN DAY AFTER BIRTH. A tropical month is the time between two passages of the Moon over the point Aries 0. The average figure is 27 days 7 hours 43 minutes 4.7 seconds.

The easiest way to calculate them is to use Julian Day numbers. Michael Erlewine in Ann Arbor, Michigan publishes a heliocentric ephemeris called *The Sun is Shining* which contains the Julian Day numbers.

It is important to remember that they are given for noon at Greenwich. If the native was born, say, at 4 a.m. in the Eastern United States, this would be 9 a.m. G.M.T. and the Julian Day would be the previous day plus 21/24 or .75 of a day.

Divide the days between birth and the event, plus the fractions of a day, by 27.3175 and add this number to the Julian Day of birth with its fraction. Thus the tertiary date is obtained. The time will be very close to the true time, which can be calculated by Chester Kemp's method using the difference between the transiting Moon and natal Moon. This distance is then turned into time. Three hundred and sixty degrees equates to 24 hours. The time is added to the time of birth, as before.

I use midpoints and the 90 degrees dial with all these methods.

Solar arc progressions are probably the most commonly used progressions by American astrologers. All natal planets have the same arc added, the arc of the Sun progressed by the day for a year measure, the usual measure for secondaries. They do not seem logical to me. However, people who use them claim that they work. In this series of cases, I have only shown them once, in *A Slight Case of Murder.*

I use converse directions, as well as direct. There seems to be a more fatal effect in directions which are produced by subtracting rather than adding. Alexander Marr, a great expert who has spent many years in meticulous research, has concluded that illnesses and death are better shown by converse directions.

I use solar returns, both sidereal and tropical. Again I cite Marr, who finds tropical returns equate to events and sidereal returns equate to psychological states.

I also use sidereal lunar returns.

All these methods failed in the New York suicide tests. Two sets of twenty charts were sent to participants. Each set contained ten charts of suicides, and ten charts matched as closely as possible in time. The date and method of suicide were given.

One sidereal solar return had Sun conjunct Jupiter close to the Moon in the tenth house. Ten days later, he killed himself. There is clearly no way of predicting events, no matter what methods are used. There is also the old rule that whatever is done at a particular time has the qualities of that time. Geoffrey Cornelius spoke to a meeting of the British Astrological Association on the *Mantric Dimension of Astrology.* He pointed out that a chart which was thought to be the genuine one could be used as if it were, and the conclusions arrived at were the same as if it had been the genuine one. Presumably, the controls and cases of the New York suicide cases were chosen at the same time, and were uncannily similar.

No one did very well on the New York suicide tests using ordinary methods. Charles Emerson did best using Uranian astrology.

Parts Of The Body

It does not need a great deal of insight to realize that the traditional assignments of the parts of the body to the signs are probable wrong. I have my own thoughts, based on the functions of the organs, which were not known when Ptolemy wrote the *Tetrabiblos*, upon which much of astrology is still based:

THE LIVER

Storage of glycogen	Moon
Manufacture of clotting factors of the blood	Saturn
Detoxifications of ingested poisons	Jupiter
Manufacture of bile	Sun
Converting indirect bilirubin to direct	Jupiter and Sun

The Mars-Saturn midpoint is connected with hemophilia, in which the liver does not manufacture the antihemophilic factor, Factor VIII.

THE PANCREAS

Production of insulin	Jupiter

Production of pancreatic enzyme, which aids in the digestion of fat. The Sun, which rules digestive enzymes. Proteins are also split by pancreatic juice into polypeptides and the Sun rules this action.

THE KIDNEY

Production of hemopoietic factor	Sun, Mars
Exchange of potassium for sodium	Venus
Maintaining fluid balance of the body	Venus, Moon
Maintaining acid-base balance of the body	Venus

The filtration of essential substances such as glucose, and return to the blood of these, and excretion of harmful substances and urea are all ruled by Venus. The secretion of renin and consequent hypertension are ruled by Mars.

ADRENALS

Production of adrenalin	Mars
Production of cortisol	Venus
Production of aldosterone	Moon
Androgens and estrogens	Mars, and Venus

THE SPLEEN

In its capacity as a storage organ	Moon
In its function of destroying red blood cells	Mars
In its function of blood formation	Mars and Moon

Neptune is the ruler in the spleen's function of producing immunocompetent lymphocytes. It is probable that the spleen is an endocrine organ. The substance, if any, which it secretes has not been identified. It may have a hormonal effect on the bone marrow. Mercury would presumably rule this function. We suspect that there are functions of the spleen which have not been discovered.

THE OVARIES

Production of estrin	Venus
Production of progesterone	Mars

The production of ova is probably ruled by Pluto, which is now known to have a great effect on the process of menstruation, together with the Moon.

THE TESTES

Production of spermatozoa	Pluto
Production of testosterone	Mars

THE PROSTATE

(Another organ whose function is largely unknown.)
Production of prostaglandins   Probably Pluto

THE PITUITARY GLAND

a) The anterior pituitary: The anterior pituitary regulates the production of cortisol, growth hormone, the gonadal steroids, thyroxine, prolactin, and probably others. It is usually given the rulership of Uranus.

b) The posterior pituitary: The main function is the production of antidiuretic hormone. This, since it regulates the body fluid and balances input and output, is under Venus.

THE PINEAL GLAND

The pineal gland is the old cyclops' third eye, our biological time-clock. No one knows the function of the pineal, although it has something to do with sexual development, and it also produces a hormone akin to certain psychedelic substances such as L.S.D. It is one of the most active amine secretors of the body.

It is said that a medical student, when asked by his instructor the function of the pineal, replied, "Sir, I have forgotten." "Gentlemen," said the professor, "this is a real tragedy for medicine. Only one man in the world knew the function of the pineal, and he has forgotten."

There is a hypothesis that schizophrenia may be due to a disordered pineal. The pineal is usually given to Neptune.

STOMACH

As a storage organ, it is rule by the Moon.
As a manufacturer of gastric juice, it is ruled by the Sun.

BREASTS

Probably Pluto as well as the Moon.

THYROID GLAND

I consider Mercury, not Venus to be the ruler of the thyroid gland. It may also be ruled by Uranus.

PARATHYROIDS

Saturn is the ruler of the parathyroids. They control the calcium metabolism.

THE COLON

Pluto rules the colon. It is here that the water from the bowel is absorbed into the blood, and the waste products ready for excretion are held until being passed on to their final storage place, the rectum.

Spastic colitis, a common affliction in which the sufferer has abdominal pain, is caused by anxiety which is suppressed, and is one of the most common psychological or autonomic nervous system disorders.

THE BLADDER

The Moon rules the bladder and other storage organs.

This scheme is sketchy and incomplete, for there is yet a great deal to be discovered. For example, there are four hundred enzymes manufactured by the liver.

However, it is a starting place. I must emphasize that nothing must be taken from the old sources, but each case must be studied to see if the principles I have set forward are correct, and if exceptions are found, new hypotheses must be formulated to account for them.

Do Biorhythms Work?

Biorhythms do not work in my chart, but that does not mean that they are of no value. There is great interest in them among astrologers, and many articles in the literature discourse on their value.

This interest has even reached the medical profession. In the psychiatric literature a study appeared recently to test the validity of the commonly used cycles, the 23 day, 28 day, and 33 day. Shaffer and Schmidt in *Archives of General Psychiatry*, no. 35 state, "In view of the implications of such a theory for both public health and safety, data from 205 carefully investigated highway crashes in which the drivers were clearly at fault were used. The authors computed specific points in drivers' biorhythm cycles at which the accidents occurred. The observed frequency of accidents occuring during the so-called critical and minus periods were then compared with the frequencies to be expected on a chance basis alone. The results provided no evidence for a relationship between purported biorhythm cycles and accident liability."

Donald Bradley studied biorhythms in a very ingenious way. He used the results of Nat Fleischer's catalogue of Famous Rematches in prize fighting. There were twenty men who had two fights each, each fighter winning one fight and losing one. The biorhythms came out 50%-50%. That is, in half the cases in which they showed the boxer should win, he lost.

He also tested the charts of forty clergymen with two events. One event was death, and one event was ordination.

The biorhythmist studied the pairs to see which of the charts showed death. Twenty-four were wrong, and sixteen were right.

Four hundred subjects whose birth and death data were recorded were also studied. The twenty-three day cycle alone was used, and the results were distributed randomly with no deviation from average values.

The twenty-three day cycle is that which is concerned with physical strength, endurance, energy, and resistance. Advocates of biorhythms offer many instances of death, heart attacks, and strokes on critical days, but even though Donald Bradley allowed for a two day leeway, just as many people died on non-critical as on critical days.

Michael Munkasey is without a doubt one of the most talented astrologers in the country. He is not only very intuitive, but is also a fine mathematician, and these qualities are not often found together. In a recent issue of *The Mercury Hour* he wrote that he connected biorhythms with the planets, and that he had intuitively divined that there were many more than the three which are customarily used. He equates the Sun with the twenty-three day cycle, and Moon with the twenty-eight day, and Mercury with the thirty-three day. The others are as follows:

Lilith	12 day cycle
Venus	36 day cycle
Mars	40 day cycle
Jupiter	45 day cycle
Saturn	52 day cycle
Uranus	58 day cycle
Neptune	63 day cycle
Pluto	70 day cycle
Psyche	76 day (the hypothetical ruler of Libra)
Transpluto	83 day cycle (the hypothetical ruler of Virgo)

Dr. Swoboda, the originator of the theory, thought that the important days to consider were those on which the cycle goes from a down phase to an up phase or at the halfway point where it changes its direction.

I calculated all the biorhythms for the New York suicide cases for which I had twenty cases and twenty controls. My results did not confirm the validity of the theory. I used those which were exact within twenty-four hours (the end of the cycle), and those which were halfway along the cycle within twelve hours.

The results were as follows:

Using only the twenty-three day cycle, seven of the twenty suicides and two of the twenty controls were critical.

Using the twenty-eight day (lunar) cycle, which might be expected to be prominent in cases of suicide, four of the suicides and two of the controls were critical.

Using the fifty-eight day (Uranus) cycle, one of the suicides and four of the controls were critical.

I am no statistician, but using a day before and after the calculated day, plus one in the middle of the cycle, means that four out of twenty-three days are considered critical in the first cycle, and one would expect around seven cases among forty by chance, so I do not consider that the results support the theory of biorhythms.

Of course, this does not mean that the planetary influences are not at their maximum at this time. For example, one of the suicide cases has the twenty-three day cycle exactly on the day of death, with the natal Sun in the 8th house and therefore a death significator.

Another has the Moon in the 2nd house, and the twenty-eight day lunar cycle is operative at death. There are no planets in the 8th house.

Another with the twenty-three day cycle operative has the Sun in the 4th house, another 'death' house.

On the other hand, one of the suicides has the Sun in Aries, the sign of his exaltation, a mere two degrees above the Ascendant and therefore very powerful. There are no biorhythms which are in a critical phase on that day, and I calculated all ten for each of the ten recognized planets.

I have learned during the course of my astrological studies to take nothing as proved unless I have proved it myself.

A Few Words About Harmonics

The new concepts about harmonics are only in their infancy, and are not understood by the majority of astrological students. Their study gives one such insight into the many problems of our art that everyone should be familiar with them.

I have used harmonics in my work since the breathtaking book by John Addey, published in 1976, explained many matters which had previously been so puzzling.

They are based on number symbolism. Briefly, John Addey found that all relationships between astrological factors had a meaning, which was related to the meaning of the number on which they were based. A few examples will make this clear.

The three hundred and sixty degree circle is divided by four to give us the square aspect. This is said by tradition to indicate difficulties in the matters represented by the two bodies forming the aspect.

If three hundred and sixty is divided by seven, we find an aspect of fifty-one degrees twenty-five minutes and forty-three seconds. This aspect is not recognized as having any meaning, but is, in fact, powerful, connected with one's creations and creativity, with inspiration and one's receptivity to it. The direction in which inspiration is sought and our capacity to focus it in our work and impart it to others is represented by the seventh harmonic. The closest solar aspect in the chart of Winston Churchill was a septile (the seventh harmonic aspect) of 51° 08' between his Sun and Mars. This accords well with his life.

It is probable that each planet is loosely connected with a special harmonic. The correlation usually given is two for the Moon, three for Jupiter, four for Uranus, five for Mercury, six for Venus, seven for Neptune, eight for Saturn, nine for Mars.

According to Addey, the number thirteen suggests the breaking out of, disturbance, or transcending of an established order of things. It is an important and not well understood harmonic. I have found that it is connected with the idea of death and regeneration. A strong thirteenth harmonic seems to give one the power to rise above one's circumstances.

Addey has found that the harmonic chart of the year of age seems to represent the conditions of the life during that year. He quotes the case of Gerald Ford, who became Vice President of the United States when he was sixty years old. The sixtieth harmonic chart is striking. Pluto is on the midheaven, and the Sun is on the seventh cusp. These charts have a potential value in rectification.

I have used the thirteen harmonic chart in several of my cases, including Chapter 21: *Knowledge is Power*.

The charts are easy to calculate. One multiplies each factor, Planet, Node, Ascendant and Midheaven, by the number and subtracts three hundred sixty until a number less than three hundred and sixty is found. A pocket calculator is invaluable for this.

The ninth harmonic or *Navamsa* has always been used in India, where it is accorded even more importance than the natal chart. If a planet is in its debility in the *Navamsa*, it is considered debilitated, even though it may be in a dignity in the natal chart. The Hindus use the sidereal zodiac, and dignities are important in their system. It is not my intention, however, to discuss harmonics in this short book, and I refer you to the work of Addey and others.

I leave the reader here, to present a series of cases of patients whose illnesses have been of great importance in their lives. They have all taught me something, and some of them have been helped by me in return. Astrology is not a sterile scientific study, to be learned out of books, but a living symbolic art, which works out in life in many varied ways.

I am indebted to all the human beings whose cases follow.

The Royal Curse

Stuart is the eldest of three sons, all of whom are hemophiliacs. This is one of the worst hereditary diseases because it is painful and crippling when hemorrhage occurs into the joints, fatal when it occurs into the brain, always threatening, causing psychological as well as physical problems, and present from birth until death.

It is an ancient curse. We read in the Bible that if the first-born son should die of uncontrollable bleeding at circumcision, the other sons may be excused from the operation. This points to the knowledge of hemophilia among the ancient Jews.

Astrologically, I would expect it to be shown by an emphasis on the 2-8 axis, that of maintaining homeostasis in the organism. The blood does not clot when it is circulating around the body, but clots when injury and bleeding threaten life. There is a long chain of factors responsible for clotting, each activated by the preceding factor. There are two kinds of hemophilia, one due to lack of factor 8 and one due to lack of factor 9. The clotting factors are made by the liver, but I place them under Saturn, not Jupiter.

This boy has Venus, the ruler of his 6th house (congenital disease) placed in Capricorn, a sign of Saturn, in the 2nd house. When the ruler of the 7th house is also the ruler of the 6th, there is sure to be a life-long hereditary disorder; this is the case here. The diagnosis of hemophilia was made soon after birth. He bled profusely at circumcision.

Charles Harvey, who studied those descendants of Queen Victoria who had inherited hemophilia, found two important degree areas, which were directly or by square aspect tenanted in each of the victims for four generations. Sometimes a midpoint fell there.

I wondered if these areas were specific for hemophilia. They are 28 Pisces 46, and 8 Aries 10.

Stuart has the Saturn-Uranus midpoint in 8 Libra 13. This has to do with the inhibition of normal rhythms-in fact, the function of the 2-8 axis which controls normal rhythms is disturbed.

The Sun-Node midpoint is close to the other sensitive point, as it falls in 28 Sagittarius 51.

This is not a fortunate chart for health.

The Pluto-Neptune midpoint is at 1 Libra 13, close to Jupiter and square the 8th cusp. It is said by Ebertin to signify a lack of will power for the maintenance of health.

Uranus, the Sun, and the Ascendant are parallel, and Venus is parallel Pluto, another indication of a serious hereditary disorder.

A normal parent would keep a child quiet and seek to educate him in the dangers of his condition. These parents were different. They seemed rather to encourage Stuart and his brothers to do everything a normal child would do. He had a large and fast sled when he was five, and each spill from it meant a couple of days in hospital. Later, he had a bicycle, a trail bike, and a snowmobile. He was encouraged to stand up for his rights at school, which meant many a bloody nose, and he was in hospital on the average six times a year. The treatment is unbelievably expensive, and as no one can afford to pay several thousand dollars a year to stay alive, the State paid all the bills, and now that he is an adult, he may find it difficult to get medical insurance. He graduated from high school last year and is still seeking employment.

The parents were divorced about seven years ago. His mother never took any responsibility for his health, and it was always his father who brought him to the office. Stuart now lives with his mother, and I have lost touch with the family, but I hear that his joints have been affected by old hemorrhages and that he will probably become crippled. He is, as far as one can tell, psychologically normal, but hemophilia is a very, very hard disease to endure.

STUART

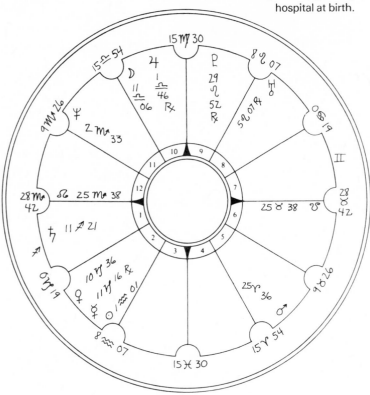

43N 39
70W 16

Born Jan. 21, 1957
2.46 a.m. E.S.T.
Family record, given by
hospital at birth.

Declinations
Sun 19 S 56
Moon 7 S 43
Mercury 20 S 01
Venus 22 S 35
Mars 10 N 30
Jupiter 0 N 34
Saturn 20 S 28
Uranus 19 N 37
Neptune 10 S 43
Pluto 22 N 06

Placidus,
calculated by Neil Michelson.

SYNOPSIS

1. The Sun is in hard aspect to the three outer planets, being opposition Uranus, square Neptune and quincunx Pluto.

He is, however, trine Jupiter, a very life-preserving aspect.

2. The second house is emphasized. The Sun, Venus and Mercury are all here, and the Moon is square Venus and Mercury, from a sign of Venus.

3. The Moon is considered to be the general ruler of fluids in the body. The Moon is waning, robbing her of some of her power. There is a sextile to Saturn, and the Moon is in the eleventh house, that of Society, indicating that Society has behaved in a responsible manner in looking after him.

4. Venus, the natural ruler of homeostasis or balancing the fluids and electrolytes of the body, is the ruler of the sixth house, and also the seventh, showing the likelihood of some hereditary disease. She conjuncts a retrograde Mercury, which shows his foolishness in not looking after himself. The influence of the house ruled is transferred to the house occupied. The sixth house influence is therefore transferred to the house ruling homeostasis.

5. According to Ebertin, the Nodes rule the joints. The Nodes are concerned with connections. They are in the 6-12 axis, pointing out the close connection during the life with illness and hospitals. They are squared by Pluto.

6. No less than four planets, including the Sun and Uranus, who are in mutual reception, occupy the 2-8 axis. Sun and Uranus are the natural rulers of the circulation.

7. The parallel between Venus and Pluto indicates that the condition is deep-seated and probably incurable.

A Fateful Eclipse

Tradition tells us that eclipses are important, and they usually signify something which is fated and cannot be changed. It has been postulated that the magnetic field of the Earth is altered at this time, and that some kind of energy which the Earth generates is cut off.

Eclipses have also traditionally been associated with blindness, and the case of the infant Donald supports the tradition. The baby was born with an extremely rare condition—he had a tumor derived from the optic chiasma nerve tissue, an astrocytoma, and became blind when he was only two months old. Before he died at the age of five months, a CT scan had demonstrated that the tumor filled two-thirds of his brain.

Donald seemed to be a normal infant at birth, and it was only towards the end of January when he was just over two months that his right eye began to bulge. It was obvious that something was pushing it forward, and he was admitted to the hospital for investigation.

On February 3rd, he was taken to the operating room for a biopsy of the tumor. When the diagnosis was made, he was sent to Boston for treatment. It was irradiated in an effort to palliate his condition, for he appeared to be in great pain.

He was not expected to live more than a week or two, but the radiation eased his pain, and he lived until April 29th. This was the anniversary of the eclipse before birth, when his mother had been about three months pregnant. Modern investigators have found that if a child is born with a malefic

DONALD

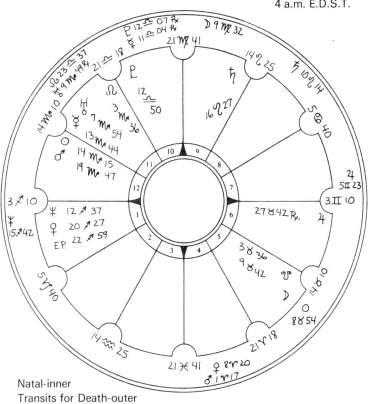

43N 39
70W 16

Born Nov. 6, 1976;
8.07 a.m. E.S.T.
Died April 29, 1977;
4 a.m. E.D.S.T.

Natal-inner
Transits for Death-outer

Declinations

	Natal	Transiting
Sun	16S 07	14N 29
Moon	14N 12	3N 38
Mercury	15S 46	16N 22
Venus	24S 43	5N 47
Mars	17S 46	0S 35
Jupiter	18N 32	20N 40
Saturn	16N 36	18N 38
Uranus	13S 42	14S 19
Neptune	20S 51	21S 09
Pluto	10S 10	11N 21

Calculated by Neil Michelson.

of the prenatal eclipse on an angle, either by conjunction or parallel of declination, the child will not survive. The eclipse planets seem to be sensitive points, which can be activated when planets transit them or when progressed planets conjunct or oppose them. South Node eclipses are considered particularly evil.

The eclipse point of the eclipses before birth should be placed in the chart and studied.

The birth Ascendant at 3 Sagittarius 10 is parallel Neptune at the time of the eclipse, and therefore, according to the rule, the child would not be expected to survive.

There are a few useful rules which indicate whether a child will be likely to die in infancy.

The Sun and Moon must both be afflicted. Saturn here parallels the Sun, and Uranus the Moon.

Fixed stars often afflict the Sun, Moon, or both. Here the Southern Scales are conjunct the Sun in the 12th house. According to Ebertin, "A bad omen is given for the health of the native if Sun or Moon is in conjunction with the Southern Scales at 14 Scorpio 23."

The Ascendant ruler is usually afflicted. Jupiter is in this case the Ascendant ruler and is placed in the 6th house, that of congenital disease, and afflicted by the parallel of Mars.

The twelfth house holds the eclipse of April 29, 1976. The poor baby spent most of his short life in hospital.

The transits at death indicate a brain death since the 1-7 axis and their rulers are involved. Jupiter, ruler of the 1st house, is parallel natal Neptune, and Mercury, ruler of the 7th house, is square transiting Saturn and opposition transiting Uranus.

The eclipse degree is held by the Moon at birth, and at death, the Sun transits it, opposed by Uranus and squared by Saturn.

It was a South Node eclipse, and the old tradition, in this case at least, appears to be true.

The Finger Of God

*"If I should pass the tomb of Jonah
I would stop there and sit for a while
Because I was swallowed one time deep in the dark
And came out alive after all."*

I first met Tim when he was four years old. He had been brought to the pediatric clinic by his mother, whose hobby was her children's health.

He had *otitis media* every time I saw him, and was becoming deaf. I could not cure it with antibiotics, but finally had a gamma globulin electrophoresis and found that his *Ig A* was extremely low.

This is not especially rare, as it occurs in about one out of six hundred children. It was treated with injections of gamma globulin, and probably this saved his hearing from permanent damage.

He was a handsome child, sturdy and well-knit, with blonde hair and blue eyes. Psychologically, he obviously was not normal. He did not play with other children, though four is a very social age. I thought he might be autistic. He had an older sister and a younger sister who played together, but Tim always played alone.

Extensive psychological testing was done. The clinic psychologist estimated his I.Q. as "low, borderline normal." He was not an easy child to test, as he refused to co-operate, and it was thought that the result showed psychological problems rather than low intelligence. Indeed this later proved to be the case.

Tim's mother obviously adored him, but his home life at that time was unsettled for his parents had just separated. It seemed there would be no more children. A baby had been stillborn about six months before I met Tim, and his mother had been found to have pre-invasive carcinoma of the cervix.

You might say that he was a behavior problem from birth. His mother maintained strict discipline, and she was not averse to giving the children a sharp slap if they stepped out of line, but Tim merely sulked and refused to be co-operative unless he felt like it. His feelings were so hidden that it was impossible to know what he really thought.

Two years later when he went to school, his I.Q. was found to be around 115 to 120. In spite of this, he did poorly at school. He would not do his homework. He failed every course. As was the custom, he got a 'social promotion' to the next grade every year.

Things got tougher as he grew older. The family was very poor, and subsisted on A.D.C. payments after the divorce. Tim refused to go to school unless he had new clothes like all the other children. Finally, they moved to another district where his mother hoped he could begin again.

It became obvious that he was having seizure activity when he was around ten or eleven years of age. There was no loss of consciousness, but there was the blank expression and fits of rage which are characteristics of temporal lobe or psychomotor seizures.

These are the worst kind. Not only are they difficult to control, but the psychomotor epileptic is likely to become violent in one of the spells, and later on have no recollection of whatever he might have done. Murders have been known to be commited during psychomotor seizures. Michael Crichton, the medical author, has written a best seller around this theme. At one time the recommended treatment was to do a lobectomy. This cured the patient, but turned him into a zombie. Since human rights have become more respected, the question has arisen as to how a criminally insane person can give informed consent for such an operation, and the procedure has fallen into disuse.

The school put him on probation when he was twelve. His mother was to rent a bellboy from the telephone company so that she could be summoned at any time to take him home from school, and she had to take him for psychological counselling every week.

Meanwhile, his mother re-married, and the home became more stable. It would have been better for Tim if she had married an older man, but his new stepfather was only eighteen years older than Tim, and young for his years. He was a poor role model. His mother was the dominant partner.

When he was thirteen, he was finally expelled. He attended school for only six weeks of the year. As the school could no longer cope with his violent behavior, they tried to place him in a "special educational facility" where the classes were smaller. His mother refused to allow him to attend when she found that all the children were retarded. It seemed that there was nowhere in the state where Timmy could be sent to get the education he needed, so he stayed at home. It must have been a bleak year, to find himself totally rejected.

In May 1976 better times came. The family bought four acres in the country, and Tim's stepfather, who is a carpenter, built a house and barn with Tim's help. The local school has small classes and special programs for children with short attention spans. The classes last only twenty minutes, and there are frequent field trips.

His sisters have horses, and he has a steer which he is raising as a 4H project. It seems that Tim is well on his way to becoming a useful citizen.

His chart shows many planets in negative signs, and the Sun is in Cancer in the twelfth house.

For diseases, we look at the Ascendant and the sixth house and their rulers, and find them to be the Sun and Saturn. Saturn is well placed; angular and in one of his own signs, but in an aspect of great tension to the Moon and Neptune in the 4th house. This tells us that his early childhood had a great deal to do with his behavior problem.

The feminine part of his nature is not able to be expressed. He is terribly vulnerable, and terribly afraid of being hurt. He suppresses his feelings. Saturn is showing its power on a deep psychological level. The Moon has an outlet which releases the tension of the square on a physical level and is trine the East Point. His unconscious is apparently breaking through and causing the psychomotor seizures.

The chart is dominated by the Y formation or Yod between Jupiter in the ninth house, Mars in the second, and the Moon and Neptune in the fourth. Two planets are in sextile, but both are 150 degrees from the third, the apex. This configuration is called by astrologers "The Finger of God" because it means that the forces symbolised by the planets involved must be integrated into the personality, and if they are not, there will be grave trouble. It is often associated with some kind of physical malfunction, and the 150 degree aspect is one of the most powerful in medical astrology.

Any planet or midpoint between two planets which is in aspect to any of the planets of the Yod will be used to bring about the effects, and in Tim's case, psychomotor epilepsy is a manifestation of the uncontrolled power of Mars.

The midpoint of the Sun and Saturn, rulers of the health of the body, is 1 Taurus, which is in 135 degree aspect to Mars. This aspect is one of the most important in medical astrology. Mars is said to be of the nature of the semisquare and Saturn of the square, and the 135 degree aspect combines the natures of both.

Epilepsy in its many forms is shown by connections between Neptune, Uranus and Mercury. Jupiter in the *Yod* is 135 degrees from Uranus, and Neptune is part of the *Yod*. The midpoint of Mercury and Neptune is semisquare the East Point.

The North Node of the Moon is in the twelfth house, bringing him into contact with illness. When life is too much for him, he is apt to retreat into psychosomatic afflictions.

The emphasis in water and the twelfth house shows a very sensative soul who has suffered very much. He has lacked a male model and does not know how to behave like a man. He is very ambivalent, being violent at times, and at other times loving and gentle.

I think that Tim was deeply hurt by the poverty of his family when he was a young child. Leo rising gives great pride, and there is a strong emphasis on the second house, showing attachment to things. At the present time, his steer is the most important thing in his life. Having worked and earned the money to buy it has done wonders for him. Jupiter is at present in his Sun sign, and he has a new home and friends, and at last things are going his way.

TIM

43N 39
70W 16

Born July 2, 1963;
7.26 a.m. E.D.S.T.
(from mother)

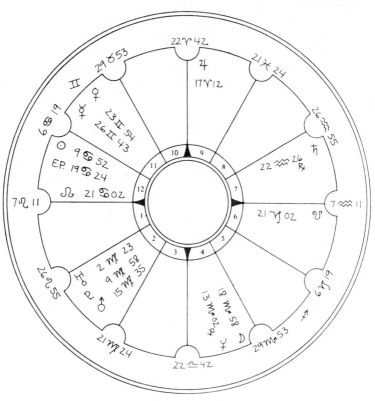

Declinations
Sun 23N 03
Moon 13S 13
Mercury 23N 07
Venus 22N 51
Mars 6N 26
Jupiter 5 N 33
Saturn 15 S 12
Uranus 0N 44
Neptune 13S 56
Pluto 20N 12

Placidus,
calculated by Neil Michelson.

SYNOPSIS

1. The key to this otherwise good chart is the *Yod* formation between Jupiter in the ninth house, Mars in the second house, and Neptune and the Moon in the fourth house.

This is the source of his life long problem, and we can see how the poverty of his early environment was a factor, since Saturn is square the Moon-Neptune conjunction.

Mars in the house of homeostasis shows that the homeostasis of the brain is disturbed, which indeed we know to be the case.

2. Saturn, very powerful in this chart, because angular, in his own sign, and retrograde, rules the sixth house. His problem is lasting, but curable, or at least treatable. He responds well to medication.

The seizures began when the progressed Sun came to the quincunx of Saturn.

3. Epilepsy is usually shown by aspects between Neptune, Mercury and Uranus. Mercury is in good aspect to Saturn, still, Saturn is showing his malefic power. Uranus does not appear to be involved.

4. The Yod discharges its energy through the empty point opposite Jupiter, which is 17 Libra in the third house.

The degree area 17 Aries-Libra is associated with violence, and has great destructive potential. In his case, it affects his mind ruled by the 3-9 axis.

An Old-Fashioned Treatment
For An Old Affliction

Severe skin disease is psychologically destructive. It can lead to untold misery in a sensitive adolesent, and it is an almost universal affliction. Michael would be good-looking but for a blotchy angry-looking eruption on his face, chest, and back, which flares up with renewed intensity every time he wants to look his best. We know that it is aggravated by stress. The sight of his face, back, and chest covered with scars and pustules is really quite dreadful, and no one knows how to treat it, for it is thought to be due to an imbalance of the glands, and who would want to interfere with the surging hormone tide of youth?

Cornell says of acne, "A Sun and Mars disease, which is due to the inflammation of sebaceous glands from retained secretions. Indications are, the Sun afflicted in Aries, the Sun square or opposition Moon or the Sun square or opposition Ascendant at birth or by direction. Afflictions in cardinal signs, as such signs indicate the skin. Saturn afflicted in Aries or Taurus as Saturn tends to retention and disordered function of the glands of the skin of the face." Donald Bradley wrote that acne would be exacerbated when Saturn and Venus appeared in the foreground of a solar or lunar return. Speaking medically, it is known that certain steroid hormones, particularly those which are androgenic, from the testis and adrenals, predispose to acne. There is often a premenstrual flare in girls associated with a preponderance of progesterone, which has a structure akin to the male hormone testosterone, at that time in the cycle. Cortisone treatment is well known to predispose to acne. It has been recommended that feminising hormone treatment be used in a desperate case. Sun-Mars therefore seems much more probable as an astrological indicator than Saturn-Venus.

The chart shows a strong emphasis on Fire. The Ascendant and M.C. are in fire signs, and the Sun rises with Mercury and Uranus. Mars is in the second house, which is said by Edith Wangemann to rule the face. Saturn is strong in his own sign on the cusp of the sixth house, and retrograde, making him even stronger. Saturn rules the skin, and is the strongest planet in the chart. This young man is a very masculine type, good with his hands and not at all interested in affairs of the mind. He is a football player, and his best subject at school is shop. He is interested in stock-car racing and motors, and will become a mechanic.

All planets are below the Earth. He is unassuming, and not at all like the usual subject with such an emphasis on Leo. The Moon in Scorpio makes him rather reserved.

There are four planets in Earth, and most are in fixed signs. He gives the impression of being a steady and reliable character. The progressed Midheaven in his eighteenth year has passed into Taurus, and is in trine to Saturn and Pluto. He is working part time, and going to school part time, and the medical treatment is helping his skin.

A skin specialist had been treating Michael for two years with no benefit before he came to me. His acne was becoming worse, and great boils had begun to appear. Even the newest drug Minocin, a tetracycline which penetrates fatty tissue and therefore can get into the sebaceous glands, did not help. Neither did a restricted diet with no chocolate, fried foods or peanut butter, and minimal dairy products. Neither did zinc. Neither did Sebulex shampoos daily and meticulous skin care, with phisohex washes and benzyl peroxidase. Neither did vitamin A, either taken by mouth or applied to the skin as an acid. I could only keep it under control by acupuncture, which works in a way no one can understand, by regulating the autonomic nervous system.

Shortly after Michael's eighteenth birthday, which occured in the summer when he was working outside and could be expected to improve with the fresh air, ultraviolet light, and drying effect of the sun—as acne sufferers usually do—his immune system seemed to break down, and he became secondarily infected with staphylococci. In desperation I turned to a very old treatment, one which was used to increase the immunity of the body by giving small initial doses of staph toxoid subcutaneously and increasing the amount every three days. This caused a tremendous local reaction, with flaring and swelling of the skin where the injection had been given, and it was obvious that he was extremely sensitive to it. The pustules, however, dried up and no new ones formed. His skin was badly scarred, but was free of infection for the first time in years.

It is interesting that the eighteenth harmonic position of Saturn is 16 Libra 12. John Addey finds that the harmonic corresponding to the age (he is now eighteen) correlates strongly with the conditions in the life at that age. Saturn comes to an exact conjunction with the fourth cusp, and is sextile to natal Uranus, perhaps showing "help from unorthodox treatment."

The indications for the breakdown of immunity have not been defined astrologically. The Moon in Scorpio, which here rules the twelfth house, may be one of them, because the twelfth is very important in immunity. The Moon is in her fall and is in paran aspect to Mars, since when she rises in the latitude of birth, Mars will be on the midheaven. A mundane square such as this is very powerful. There is a great deal of fire and a great deal of Mars influence in the chart. Fixed signs, especially when rising, indicate hereditary tendencies to diseases of excess, particularly diabetes and hypertension. In this family there is a spirit of cheerful hedonism. They are sociable, gregarious, and find a great deal of pleasure in eating and drinking. His grandmother was an enormously obese woman and died at the age of sixty-two of circulatory failure complicating longstanding and uncontrolled diabetes, hypertension, and gall bladder disease. A Sun-Uranus conjunction in the first house square the Moon and Jupiter is almost certain to indicate that he will follow the family tendency.

He will probably turn out to be an alcoholic. Although he is only eighteen, he appears at the office with a hangover from

MICHAEL

43N 44
70W 20
Moon void-of-course.

Born at 4.20 a.m.
Aug. 12, 1959 E.D.S.T.
Birth data
from mother.

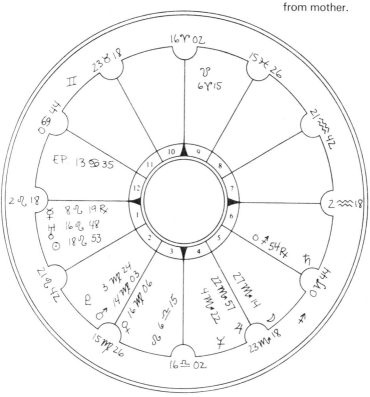

Declinations.
Sun 15N 10
Moon 15N 33
Mercury 14N 29
Venus 0N 22
Mars 7N 02
Jupiter 17N 45
Saturn 22S 36
Uranus 16N 25
Neptune 11S 20
Pluto 21N 11

Topocentric.

drinking beer all weekend. His father and mother are separated, but he sees his father several times a week, and there is great family dissension about the drinking, because his mother nags him about it constantly and his father tells him to pay no attention to her.

✓ The Moon is void-of-course. The definition of this astrological term is that the Moon has made the last major aspect it will make before it changes from one sign of the Zodiac to the next.

The Moon rules the native's ability to get along with people and his adaptability to the environment. The native with the Moon void-of-course is born totally vulnerable to his environment without any protection on the emotional level.

The emotions are not absent, but they respond in an inappropriate manner to emotional situations. It seems that the planet Neptune is prominent and important in people with a void-of-course Moon. Here Neptune is in the fourth house, that of the home and early childhood influences.

The skin is an organ which responds to stress and to psychological conditions in the environment. The impurities in the system are excreted by the eighth house and Scorpio. Here we have three planets in Scorpio, one of which is Neptune in the fourth house. It is rare that one sees such a disfiguring case of acne, and I think that his home environment has had a great deal to do with it, and that he will only be permanently improved when he leaves home.

It is not good to have all the planets in one hemisphere, and I do not think this is a fortunate chart. I suspect that Michael will have the diseases to which people who are overweight generally succumb.

An Impossible Diagnosis

It is not often that a case is so baffling that a diagnosis cannot be made, in spite of all the resources of a modern hospital.

Nicole was born at 12.12 p.m. E.D.S.T. on July 18, 1972. She died of fulminating liver and brain disease in the spring of 1977, which was diagnosed as Reye's syndrome. However, there were some findings which did not fit this diagnosis. It was felt that she might have had Wilson's disease, a familial dominant disorder. It was important to find out, as there were two other children in the family, and there is a fifty per cent chance of inheritance. Most neurological disorders are incurable and untreatable, but there is a treatment for Wilson's disease if it is diagnosed early enough.

Nicole's liver was removed at autopsy and sent to California for the copper content to be measured. It was higher than normal, as if it were indeed Wilson's disease, but not high enough to be diagnostic. I do not think that any cases of Wilson's disease have been found at such a young age. Death was from brain and liver failure, and she died in four days.

Reye's syndrome is an interesting disease. It seems not to have been recognized before 1951, and not to have been described in the literature before 1963. A pathologist in Australia whose name was Reye was puzzled by the death within two days of a child who had been healthy until she developed liver failure associated with extreme swelling and rapid dissolution of the brain. The encephalopathy came on suddenly, and there were seizures, restlessness, deepening coma and death. Although the liver function was abnormal and the blood level of ammonia, a toxic product, extremely high, there was no increase in the blood bilirubin and therefore no jaundice. After Reye had seen his first case at autopsy, he looked for others, as he recognized that no one had ever described such a disease in young children. Eleven years later, he published an account and clinical description, and the new syndrome was given his name. Reports of children with Reyes syndrome then began to appear from all over the world, and the puzzle still has not been settled as to whether it existed but was not recognized or whether it is a new disease. The cause is not known. It seems to follow certain virus infections, especially chicken pox and influenza *B*. About 50% of the patients die, and there is no specific treatment, although exchange transfusions have been tried. The cause of the liver failure and brain symptoms is not understood.

Nicole had always been healthy except that she had had headaches, beginning at the age of around two years and recurring irregularly but at least once a month. They were associated with vomiting, and were typical of childhood migraine, although there was no family history of this, and it is usually familial.

She had a headache, a fever, and vomited several times on May 7, and on May 8, when she became drowsy and her mother could not rouse her. She was admitted in coma to the hospital, and in spite of supportive measures, including an exchange transfusion, died on May 12. The only thing that did not fit Reyes' syndrome was that the bilirubin was high on admission and rose to 20 mg., which is too elevated for this diagnosis. Wilson's disease is associated with a high bilirubin, because there is liver damage due to copper being laid down in the liver. It is an inborn error of metabolism in which the body lacks an enzyme needed to metabolize copper. It is not usually diagnosed until the teens and the diagnosis is made by a biopsy of the liver, when excess copper is found.

Now to look at the chart.

An old axiom tells us that if the ruler of the first house and the ruler of the seventh are in conjunction, the life will be short. Here they are parallel, which has a similar effect.

We look to the Sun and the Moon, remembering that the Moon is particularly important to the age of seven years. The *(? 4 yrs)* Moon is parallel Pluto and the Sun is parallel Saturn. I have seen this combination many times in cases of death in childhood.

There is also a relationship in paran between the Moon and Mars at this latitude. When the natal Moon near 0 Scorpio is on the fourth cusp, Mars rises in 12 Leo 40 and a paran square is present.

Venus is the ruler of the Ascendant and eighth house. Bellatrix, a malefic fixed star, is conjunct Venus.

I believe that the sixth house shows inherited disease. Wilson's disease falls into this category. Here it is ruled by Neptune. At death, transiting Neptune is opposition natal Saturn. This indicates to me that there was an inherited disease which manifested itself at this time. It is interesting that Venus rules copper.

The liver has many functions and several rulers. This little girl died because of failure of the detoxifying function. I place this under Jupiter, which also rules the higher cerebral functions. Transiting Jupiter is 150 degrees from transiting Uranus, a dangerous aspect, especially since Uranus is in Scorpio, which rules excretion. The ammonia released in metabolism was not able to be excreted by the kidneys, and poisoned the body.

At death, there were three main configurations.

Transiting Uranus and Saturn formed a square close to the eighth cusp. This had been forming and reforming for some time.

There was an eclipse on April 4th in 14 Libra 23 on the Ascendant.

Transiting Venus and Mars are in opposition transiting Pluto. Here is the configuration which would be expected for this type of death, a brain death. The axis affected is 1-7.

After the exchange transfusion on May 11th, Nicole

stopped breathing and was put on the respirator. It was turned off at 7.30 p.m. on May 12th. There had been no electrical activity on the electroencephalogram for some hours before she was finally pronounced dead.

SYNOPSIS

1. Natal Indications of Early Death.
   Moon parallel Pluto.
   Sun parallel Saturn.
   Eclipse 8 days before birth close to M.C.
   Ruler of natal 7th house, Mars, is paran square Moon.
   Sun closely conjunct S. Node.
   Neptune ruler of 6th house-inherited disease.
   A significant midpoint is Pluto equals Moon-Neptune.
   Pluto square Jupiter.
2. Timing of Death.
   Progressed Ascendant ruler Sun, which rules bile is with Uranus, ruler of the progressed 7th.
   Progressed Mercury is parallel Pluto.
   Neptune is square progressed Ascendant, and Jupiter trine it, but square Pluto. Jupiter is also quincunx progressed Sun.
   Therefore Jupiter, Neptune and Pluto all have an association with the 1-7 axis, ruling brain death.
3. Cause of Death
   Brain failure, due to breakdown in detoxification (Jupiter) and inability to excrete poisons (Pluto).
4. Transits.
   A repetition of the assault on the 1-7 axis is seen.
   Mars conjunct Venus on the 7th cusp opposes Pluto transiting over Ascendant.
   A *Yod* formation between transiting Jupiter, Uranus and Saturn is formed, with the apex falling close to the 8th cusp.
   An eclipse on April 4, 1977 in 14 Libra 23 fell close to natal Ascendant.

NICOLE

43 N 39
70 W 16
Moon void-of-course.

Born July 18, 1972;
12.12 p.m. E.D.S.T.
(Hospital record)

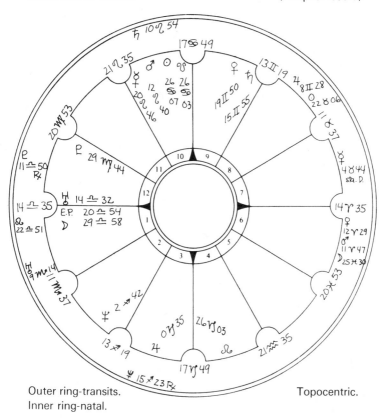

Outer ring-transits.
Inner ring-natal.

Topocentric.

Declinations	
Natal	Transits at death.
Sun 20N 56	Sun 18N 18
Moon 14S 09	Moon 0N 29
Mercury 12N 37	Mercury 10N 48
Venus 17N 54	Venus 5N 03
Mars 18N 09	Mars 3N 35
Jupiter 23S 18	Jupiter 21N 12
Saturn 21N10	Saturn 18N 27
Uranus 5S 07	Uranus 14S 08
Neptune 19S 01	Neptune 21S 07
Pluto 14S 05	Pluto 11N 24

A Slight Case Of Murder?

"Is it possible," I was asked recently, "for someone to be murdered so that it looks like a heart attack?"

I get all kinds of questions in the office, but this was a shocker. A kindly old man of sixty-nine had been found dead in his bed, apparently having died in his sleep. The medical examiner had certified that he had succumbed to a massive myocardial infarct. His grieving widow had gone into a state of shock. It seemed that his pension had died with him, and there would only be a small social security income for her, barely enough to keep body and soul together.

But did he have a heart attack? How could one tell?

The dead man had been in the Navy, and had been at sea for years and years at a time. In his absence, his wife had given birth to three children who could not possibly have been his. In fact, their father, a married man who lived in the neighborhood, used to visit her quite openly. There were also three older boys for him to support, and the money was never quite enough. The family had extinquished its debts three times by going bankrupt, but this did not seem to prevent them from getting credit. The small home was a refuge for all the family members who did not work, and at the time of his death, there were two daughters and the youngest son, now twenty-five, the husband of one daughter, the girl friend of the son, and a divorced son of thirty-four, as well as his wife and himself. He had been banished to the attic for years, and it was a mystery to everyone how they could all squeeze into the house. His wife loved to have her children around her. He worked as a chef, even though he had retired from the Navy. It was an intolerable life, and it would seem that he had a fortunate escape from it by dying quietly in his sleep.

A niece who was devoted to him was very disturbed. "I had a vivid dream last night," she began. "I was talking to my uncle. He did not seem to be dead. In fact, he was very much alive. We were talking, and yet we were not speaking in words, but seemed to know each other's thoughts. He said that he did not mind being dead, but that it had not been easy to go, because he had been murdered. 'Who would do such an awful thing?' I asked, and he said, 'It was for the pension. My wife thought that she would have the pension, and there would be more room in the house without me.'" The twenty-five year old son and the wife had smothered him when everyone else was out. "Then," she said, "my husband began to shake me, because he wanted me to wake up. I looked strange. I came back with an unpleasant jolt."

Was it a true dream and had she really been in communication with her uncle? Or was it produced by her subconscious mind? Astrology should be able to give an answer.

Fortunately, the family Bible had recorded the date and time of the wife Maude's birth. Only the date without the time of her husband Ned's birth was known.

Maude was born almost at a New Moon. This is called the Hecate phase of the Moon, and a woman who has this configuration is sure to outlive her husband. It is the Moon in her phase as a Death Goddess.

She has 8 Libra rising. This is close to Vindemiatrix, the Grape-gatherer, but sometimes known as Widow-Maker.

She was beautiful and sociable, and married young to escape from her domineering mother. Her father was no longer in the picture, having also chosen to escape, by suicide. This, in itself, may have caused the male image to have the imprint of violence. Note the dreadful conjunction of Saturn and Pluto in her 9th house.

One man was never enough for her, and this may have been the subconscious reason for choosing a Navy man, who was bound to be away from home, leaving her free to seek other entertainment. Mars conjunct Venus in Aries in the seventh house gives a nature dominated by desire for physical sensation. Mars is in his own sign, therefore strong, and overwhelms Venus. Venus rules the Ascendant and Mars the seventh, the house of the partner, and those with this combination receive cruelty or express themselves cruelly towards the partner. At any rate, this is one of the ways in which the combination can act.

The best planet in her chart, Jupiter, in Pisces where he is exalted, led to a kind of profligacy which kept the family perpetually broke. The house ran itself, as she refused to do either cooking or housework. She loved nice things, but did not care to look after them, so anyone following her to the dump was apt to find a bicycle which was almost new except that the gear shift did not function, or a set of living room furniture that had become slightly shabby. She also loved to have people around, and her children's friends were welcome at any time, to come for a meal, or stay the night if they could find an unoccupied corner. She chose a man with Saturn in close conjunction to this Jupiter, and must have always felt that he disapproved, especially since he had to pay the bills.

Her creativity was expressed through her children. Uranus in the fifth house gives unusual children or a strange and unusual upbringing. There were many of them—six living, but another six who died in infancy or were miscarried. They were brought up to live by their wits, doing little as possible. Their father seemed to have had no influence on them, and they treated him as badly as their mother did. The oldest son was married three or four times, fathered many children, and always managed to find wives who would support him.

Certainly Uranus in the fifth house square a Sun-Moon conjunction in Taurus would be expected to give intense experiences in the areas of sex, birth, money, and death, and all these were well expressed in her life.

Her husband did not share her life. He worked to support

them all, and when home was expected to do the cooking and whatever housework was done.

He had a Moon which was square Saturn and conjunct Pluto. The time of his birth is unknown, but he emigrated to the United States from Norway when he was very young. He was born in Oslo and his solar chart is given for comparison with hers.

It is unbalanced, with six planets in mutable signs. The Nodes are close to the Uranus-Neptune opposition, and Venus is near the South Node. He needed the structure of a family after his years of wandering in the Navy, and tolerated anything to be allowed to live with his wife and children.

Her solar chart shows Sagittarius on the eighth cusp, and she needs a Fire type man, preferably a Sagittarian, to fulfill her sexual needs. She also needs him to fulfill her financial needs, which, after the first three children were born, seemed more important. The eighth house, after all, is concerned with both sex and money.

Her Moon conjunct Sun in the eighth house indicates that her subconscious feminine self has an urge to dominate, and perhaps that is why the new Moon is called Hecate. There is no doubt that the feminine principle can destroy-and with the Pluto-Saturn conjunction, she is certainly cold blooded and quite amoral.

The natal chart shows possibilities only. The progressed chart shows the times at which the possibilities will become activated.

What would one expect to see if a woman murdered her husband? Saturn, representing an older man, and also someone who has a restrictive effect, should come to a prominent position in the natal or progressed chart. In this case, Saturn has progressed to the eighth degree of Cancer, almost on the midheaven and square the Ascendant-Descendant axis.

The third house of the chart represents the immediate surroundings (the neighborhood) and the opposite house, the ninth, shows the immediate surroundings of the husband. In the natal chart Mercury is closely conjunct the ninth cusp, and in the progressed chart Mars has come to this point. "Danger in the immediate surroundings of the husband."

There is a square between transiting Saturn and Uranus. Transiting Uranus is in 11 Scorpio, semisquare his natal Sun. The semisquare 45 is said to be of the nature of Mars. He was therefore at this time particularly susceptible to the effects of violence from outside, as the transits show influences directed towards the native, of an 'accidental' character.

Transiting Mars and Jupiter are in square, and if one uses the solar arc positions, where each planet is progressed by the arc moved by the secondary day for a year Sun, Mars is opposition Saturn and Pluto, and is almost exactly in their midpoint axis. Solar arc Uranus is also in opposition transiting Pluto. His natal Neptune is in this axis. Mars in hard aspect to the Saturn-Pluto midpoint means assault according to Ebertin.

The transiting Moon on the night he died is opposition solar arc Neptune, in the twelfth house of his wife, indicating some matter which is secret and hidden.

Mercury rules her natal twelfth house. The secondary progressed chart shows Mercury and Pluto in conjunction in Cancer 2. One would expect Pluto to be involved in this kind of case.

The closest aspect in Maude's secondary chart is the progressed Moon in the sixteenth degree of Leo opposition natal Uranus in the fifth house. This would excite and stimulate her, possibly to the point of frenzy. She would be quite out of control.

The Mars-Saturn midpoint in the progressed chart is at 22 Gemini square natal Jupiter. Ebertin gives the interpretation "the ability to destroy or eliminate something completely."

The aspects are too violent for a natural death. It was a true dream, and he was murdered.

The fourth house is supposed to show conditions after death. His natal Uranus is close to her fourth cusp. This leads us to wonder if there will be another chapter before the matter is closed.

He supported them all when he was alive, but in the end his luck ran out. He made quite certain that the Masons would get everything he left. His pension died with him. The son moved out to live with his girl friend. The married daughter moved out. The divorced son moved out. The youngest daughter married rather suddenly, and when her mother came home one day, she found that all the furniture had been removed, and a note from this daughter said briefly, "The furniture was mine. I paid for most of it. We have moved it to Arizona, where we have gone to start a new life." The house is now empty, except for her memories.

It seems that he has been avenged.

MAUDE

43N 39
70W 16

3 p.m. May 13, 1915
From Family Bible.

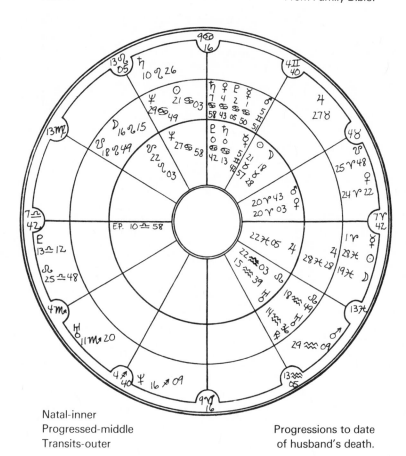

Natal-inner
Progressed-middle
Transits-outer

Progressions to date
of husband's death.

Solar Arc Planets.
Saturn, Pluto 29 Leo
Jupiter 21 Taurus
Uranus 14 Aries
Neptune 17 Virgo

NED

Solar Chart.   Dec. 19, 1907

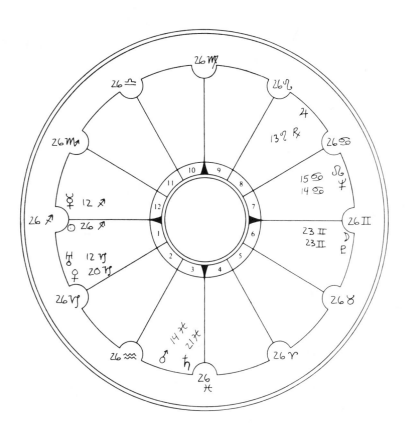

Note his wife's Neptune on the 8th cusp of his solar chart.

Never Believe A Patient

Jody was born at 3:16 a.m. on February 14, 1965 in Portland, Maine, and she almost died on May 9, 1969. I remember that evening well.

She was the youngest of three children, and the family situation when I first knew them in 1968 was chaotic. Her mother and father had recently separated, and her mother was trying to make it on very uncertain and irregular child support payments and an A.D.C. check. She had, in her way, a real talent with children, and looked after two others as well as her own. This seemed better than going out to work. Life was not easy for them.

Jody and her brother and sister lived in a roomy apartment with a small garden, and it was pin-neat, cheerful, and full of kittens and plants. I often stopped for a cup of coffee if I had to make a house call. The family had no car, and I was concerned about their many problems.

I knew the children very well. You might say that the health of her family was the mother's hobby, and they were almost weekly visitors at the pediatric clinic where I worked as part of my training. I have written about her brother Tim in Chapter 9: *The Finger of God.*

One day Jody and Johnnie, who stayed with them when his mother worked, were playing doctor and nurse. They found some pink pills in her mother's handbag, and administered them to each other. A few minutes later, Jody's mother realized that her bottle of tranquilizers was empty.

"He ate them," said Jody. "I didn't eat them... he ate them." They were put in a neighbor's car and driven to the nearest hospital. The little boy, who had a pink tongue, was given some syrup of ipecac and his stomach was washed out. Jody, who stoutly maintained that she had not had any, was given some ipecac, but did not vomit. They believed her, and did not lavage her stomach.

On the way home, she had a convulsion, and her mother took her to the other hospital, where nearly everyone had gone home for the weekend, and I was left on duty. She was becoming drowsy, and it was obvious that she would soon be in coma. The intensive care unit readied a bed and hooked up a cardiac monitor, and I called the drug company.

In theory, the big drug companies have someone available at all times to answer questions. In practice, it is not always easy to find the medical representative late on a Friday evening. By the time I reached him, Jody was deeply in coma, a suction machine by her bed to clear her lungs of mucus, a stomach tube in place, and an intravenous solution running into her veins with a vasopressor to maintain her blood pressure. A respirator was standing by in case she stopped breathing.

He had some good news and some bad news. The good news was that they had not lost a child with this kind of tranquilizer poisoning. The bad news was that the half life was around thirty-six hours, so she would certainly be in coma for two or three days.

Meanwhile, Jody began to have seizures. We did not know it at the time, but this was the beginning of her epilepsy, which later showed up in her brother also. She hung between life and death, and we had some very, very anxious moments.

The drug company representative was quite right. She did recover, as he said she would, and after four days, she was as good as new.

I still see Jody. Her mother is remarried. Her new stepfather adopted the three children. She grew tall and beautiful. She is now the proud possessor of her own horse, and she belongs to a country 4H club. They have a new house in a rural area. The family won through to better times.

Now for a look at her chart.

It is dominated by a T square in fixed signs, involving Jupiter oppostion Neptune and a stellium in the second house with Sun, Mercury, and Venus.

This sets up a pattern of severe pressure, but there is the possibility of releasing it through the trine from Jupiter to the Virgo planets.

The indication of poisoning by drugs is clearly shown.

Jupiter is the ruler of the chart, and is placed natally in the fifth house.

This is the mark of the gambler, one who is always ready to take a chance. She has great faith in life.

Neptune is in opposition from the eleventh house, the house of friends.

"Poisoning by drugs given by a friend." Sometimes the keywords seem to fit the situation in an uncannily accurate way.

By transit Neptune is in 27 Scorpio 34. This is past the square to natal Sun.

But there is another important aspect, which is not easy to find. Cyril Fagan first drew attention to the importance of mundane squares in a chart. At the latitude of Portland, Maine, 43 N 39, when 27 Scorpio 34 rises, 13 Virgo 33 is on the M.C.

There is, therefore, a mundane square between them.

Transiting Mars squares natal Uranus and Pluto.

Transiting Sun, Neptune, and Pluto are parallel natal Mercury.

Her mother is represented by Mars and the Sun. She is Mars because Mars rules the fourth cusp, and the Sun because the Sun rules Leo where the Moon is placed, and also is the subruler of the second decanate of Aries.

Her mother is the most important person in her life, she was trying to imitate her. This is why she took her pills.

Mercury is the lie she told. Mercury rules the sixth house, bringing in the epileptic seizures, since Mercury and Uranus, both important in epilepsy, are connected by being in mutual reception.

Transiting Jupiter joined natal Mars at the time she was admitted to hospital, and the transiting South node was with them. Saturn natal was on the twelfth cusp of the secondary chart. Naturally she did not die. The ninth house holding the twenty-seventh degree of Virgo is a fortunate house, linked with natal Jupiter by a trine. Her mother saved her life by quick action.

She came close to it. Coma comes under the eighth house—a death-like experience. The Sun, ruler of the eighth house, is linked with Neptune by a close parallel of the two transiting bodies on May 9th at 9 p.m. The Sun is with natal Jupiter.

We must look at the Ascendant and Ascendant ruler to find the main health problem of her life. She has severe migraine headaches as well as epilepsy.

The chart is very unbalanced. There is a preponderance of six fixed planets, and the others are in mutable signs. There is a lack of angular planets. No less than seven planets are placed in succedent houses where they are at their weakest.

What is epilepsy? It is a storm of electrical impulses in the brain associated with an altered state of consciousness. Is the ego driven out? We think so. The Sun rules the eighth and is placed in the second. The ego does not sit firmly here, especially in Aquarius, the sign of the detriment of the Sun.

The closest square is Jupiter-Mercury, invoking stress to the psychomotor channels. The ruler has two aspects which might cause us to suspect a disorder of the rhythm of the brain, for there is also the aspect to Neptune, ruler of the third house, that of the mind and communication.

The South node in the twelfth house hints that much of

the life will be spent coping with physical or metal illness, either in the self or others.

The key to the poisoning was the position of transiting Jupiter. The progressed planets show the unfolding of whatever was present at birth in the form of a seed. The transits show the accidents of life, in the form of outside pressures and temptations. Jupiter was in the twenty-seventh degree of Virgo with natal Mars in the ninth house.

The ninth house rules the brain. Jupiter is accidently dignified here, meaning that in the natural Zodiac with 0 Aries rising, Sagittarius, which is Jupiter's sign, is in the ninth.

Note that the South node of the Moon is transiting with Jupiter. This is said to be a point of self-undoing.

Consider the paran connections of 27 Virgo. In this latitude, when on the midheaven, 6 Sagittarius rises. Natal Saturn is in 6 Pisces, and when she sank into coma, the transiting Moon had reached this very degree.

The midpoint of the Ascendant and Midheaven has been called 'the point of the soul.' The soul (or ego) is driven out during an epileptic seizure, and transiting Neptune was there at the time of the onset of her epilepsy. The transiting Sun, Pluto and Neptune are all in parallel at 17-18 declination with her natal Mercury, and this indicates that at that time a deep-seated hereditary condition will manifest itself. Natal Mercury is in the second house, indicating electrolyte imbalance due to ingestion.

One wonders about the meaning of the experience to the child. She has forgotten her poisoning in her conscious mind, but they say that every deed has a far reaching effect which may not be manifest until years later. The most important degree at that time was 27 Virgo, said to signify 'disinterested service to humanity.' There was also a close contact between her chart and that of the physician who looked after her, for her Mercury is exactly conjunct my Ascendant and her 'point of soul' with transiting Neptune on my Midheaven. Perhaps it was no coincidence that I chanced to be on duty that weekend long ago.

JODY

43N 39
70W 16

Born Feb. 14, 1965;
3.16 a.m. E.S.T.
(Data from mother.)

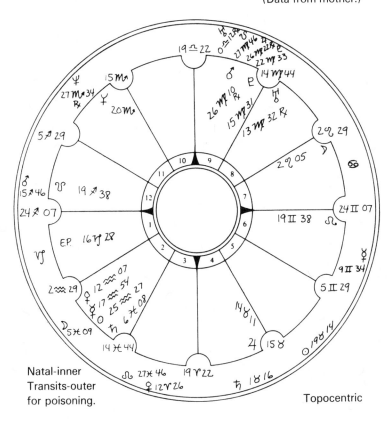

Natal-inner
Transits-outer
for poisoning.

Topocentric

Declinations Natal	Transiting. May 9, 1969; 9.10 p.m.
Sun 13S 02	Sun 17N 31
Moon 22N 56	Moon 12S 17
Mercury 17S 50	Mercury 24N 14
Venus 18S 15	Venus 5N 38
Mars 5N 04	Mars 23N 50
Jupiter 16N 24	Jupiter 2N 48
Saturn 10S 43	Saturn 9N 48
Uranus 7N 13	Uranus 17S 55
Neptune 16S 02	Neptune 17S 55
Pluto 19N 06	Pluto 17N 26

SYNOPSIS

POISONING

1. Natal T square Jupiter opposition Neptune square Sun/Mercury/Venus.
2. Transiting Neptune paran square natal Sun, ruler of eighth.
3. S. Node with Jupiter transiting natal Mars ruler of fourth.
4. Saturn conjunct twelfth cusp of seconday chart (not shown.)

EPILEPSY

1. Jupiter ruler of the Ascendant square Mercury ruler of sixth opposition Neptune ruler of third.
2. Uranus quincunx Mercury, thus aspecting the natal T square.
3. Uranus disposes of the planets in the second, Sun, Mercury, and Venus.
4. Transiting Sun, Pluto, Neptune parallel natal Mercury at first seizure.

MIGRAINE

1 Mars in Virgo in the ninth square Ascendant in Sagittarius.

Never Bet A Dollar On
A Horse Called Eternity

Bonnie was born prematurely in the North of Maine and weighed only eight hundred and fifty grams. She was at once transported about two hundred miles by helicopter to the nearest intensive care unit in Portland, where she arrived looking very vigorous, considering she was so premature. She was placed in an incubator with 30% oxygen, and put under the bilirubin lights. After twenty-four hours, she was breathing room air, and all seemed to be well.

It is important to give nourishment to these small babies as early as possible, in order to avoid brain damage from low blood sugar. Since their stomachs are too small and undeveloped to tolerate anything by mouth, routine intravenous feeding is used. On the first day, 10% dextrose is given, and then lipids, amino acids, minerals and vitamins in a special solution.

Bonnie began to vomit on the third day, and for the next four days, she was bringing up bile-stained fluid. X-rays showed no obstruction in the digestive tract, and there was no blood in the stools. Although all the cultures taken from her skin, stomach and umbilical cord were sterile, she was given a five day course of antibiotics. By the eighth day, she was much better, and could take feeding by mouth. One cc. per hour was given into a tube placed and left in her stomach, and the formula used was exactly as strong as her blood, i.e., isomolar, because this is easier to digest. Everything went well, and she became able to tolerate larger and larger amounts without vomiting.

An error of management was then made. On her sixteenth day of life, the formula was changed to a hyperosmolar one, with twenty-four calories per ounce instead of only twenty. Usually this formula is not given to an infant of this weight until the twenty-first day. The abdomen became distended, and bloody fluid could be withdrawn from her stomach. X-rays showed that her intestines had perforated.

From this time, it was downhill all the way. She was given antibiotics, alkalinising agents, positive airway pressure with a ventilator, and finally taken to the operating room where a colostomy was carried out. She went into shock, had renal shut-down, and died four days after the operation. The diagnosis: necrotising enterocolitis. The national incidence is 3-8% of admissions to neonatal intensive care units, and the mortality is around 38%. It is a disease of intestinal and gastric dysfunction.

The birthchart is a classical example of neonatal mortality. The Moon, the main indicator of death in infancy, is opposition Uranus in the third house and square Saturn in the twelfth. It is in Taurus, ruled by Venus, and Venus is with Mars in the eighth house 135 degrees from the Ascendant. This is the signature of death in infancy. The prenatal eclipse of April 4th fell in 14 Libra 23, opposite Venus and Mars. The Ascendant ruler is the Sun, which is parallel Saturn and with Algol.

At death, Jupiter stood opposition Neptune from the tenth house to the fourth. These are houses concerned with the function of nutrition, and this is the commonest of all aspects at death. The Moon was 135 degrees from Uranus and just entering the eighth house. The seventh house and the eighth house are both related to death, and the Moon has just left the square of the ruler of the eighth (Neptune) and is applying to the sesquiquadrate of the ruler of the seventh (Uranus).

I have always believed that Virgo had nothing to do with the intestines. The ruler of the colon is Pluto, and the function of elimination is ruled by the eighth house. This is the one affected by the eclipse, and death was due to intestinal dysfunction.

BONNIE

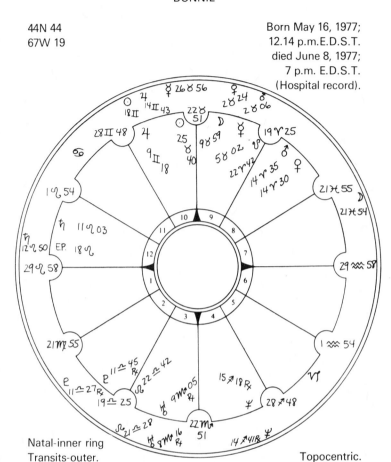

44N 44
67W 19

Born May 16, 1977;
12.14 p.m.E.D.S.T.
died June 8, 1977;
7 p.m. E.D.S.T.
(Hospital record).

Natal-inner ring
Transits-outer.

Topocentric.

Declinations.	Transiting
Natal	at death.
Sun 19N 03	Sun 22N 54
Moon 11N 12	Moon 0S 48
Mercury 10N 22	Mercury 17N 12
Venus 5N 17	Venus 9N 58
Mars 4N 32	Mars 11N 15
Jupiter 21N 19	Jupiter 22N 05
Saturn 18N 25	Saturn 17N 54
Uranus 14S 05	Uranus 13S 46
Neptune 21S 06	Neptune 21S 01
Pluto 11N 24	Pluto 11N 18

The Gorgon's Head

I do not consider this chart to be a difficult one, indeed, Flo always has been lucky. The influence of the fixed stars is not particularly easy to see, but Algol is here with the Sun, and the life has been a classical example of the evil of this star, which is called The Gorgon's Head.

She is probably the most selfish person I have ever met, and lives only to exploit others. The only thing Flo ever feared was her mother. It is certain she was suppressed in her childhood and could never show her feelings for fear of punishment. The stage was set for cancer, if we can believe those who claim that it is a psychosomatic disease.

Her father shot himself. Her brother died of hemophilia. Her sister outwardly assented to all the rules and regulations of the household but quietly went her own way. The influence of her mother on Flo was to abolish completely all tender feelings, and she is quite asexual and sternly religious in the worst possible way.

In 1962, this woman had carcinoma of the ovaries, uterus and Fallopian tubes. It is interesting and significant that the denial of love and sexuality should have taken revenge in this way. An imbalance of the normal ratio of the female hormones has been thought to be the probable cause of malignant disease of the sex organs, although this in not certain, and indeed there was a serious imbalance in this patient.

There are three planets in Taurus, which is quite typical. Flo was married at the age of twenty, because she had become pregnant. She had a daughter, whom she refused to bring up,

and she even refused to bring her home from the hospital. Her
sister looked after the baby, and later, after her sister had
married and left home, her mother adopted the child. Between
her aunt and her grandmother, the poor child had such a
oppressive time that she ran away from home at the age of
fifteen, and was self-supporting thereafter. The patient's
marriage was dissolved after only a few months. After that,
she never had any interest whatsoever in any man, and the
great mystery for all who knew her was how she got herself
impregnated at all. There were, apparently, homosexual
tendencies as she lived with a young woman for several years
and became very upset and resentful when this friend moved
out and married.

The Mars conjunct Neptune in her chart gives a kind of
Messiah complex as well as a strange sexuality. She honestly
believes that she is perfect.

The hormone imbalance is responsible for her bizarre
medical history. She had severe bleeding for about ten years
from fibroids of the uterus, themselves caused by hormone
imbalance. Finally, she lost so much blood that she became
unconscious in the street and a passer-by ordered an
ambulance to take her to the hospital. Gynecological
examination showed fibroids and a hysterectomy was
performed, but the surgeon saw cancer in the tubes and
ovaries as soon as he opened her up. During the freeing of the
enlarged tubes, one of them ruptured and seeded cancer cells
throughout the pelvic cavity. A course of cobalt treatment was
given, and there has been no recurrence in fifteen years.

I do not know the date of her operation. It was in or
around February 1962, and I have inserted the transits of
February 14th outside the natal positions.

Before her serious illness, she used to despise people who
were ill. Now she has become quite neurotic about her health.
She is always the first in line whenever any free public health
services are offered. She thinks that any bruise, any stiffness,
any thickening of the skin, any feeling of fatigue, is due to the
return of her cancer.

However, she has not learned to live life. She has no
interests except her narrow and rigid Christianity, which could

not be further from what Jesus taught. She delights in getting something for nothing and is extraordinarily lucky. Her main talent is in getting other people to help her. Last year, she obtained about fifteen cords of free firewood, and then complained because the man who delivered it did not stack it for her. She has no idea of anything that is going on in the world around her, and has never known the joy of helping someone less fortunate. This chart is a classic example of the effect of Algol. She is the prototype of the negative Virgo. Everything detrimental that has ever been said about Virgo applies to Flo.

The Sun conjuncts Saturn and Algol in the ninth house. This should have given her some depth of thought. According to Liz Greene, the kind of pain which accompanies this placement is loss of faith. The search is for a new framework by which the life can be given meaning. She has adopted a narrow religious faith of the old kind, which held that only those who were true believers could be saved and that all others would be eternally damned. Her God is Jehovah, a narrow and partisan God, a saturnine God. He does not prevent her from cheating anyone, as those who are not 'saved' are fair game.

The South Node with Fortuna in the second house may be responsible for her miserliness.

The ruler of the eighth is Neptune, and the Neptune-Mars conjunction is common in malignant disease, and is a symbol of the denial of the feminine part of her nature, which has taken such a terrible revenge. Saturn is at the midpoint of the North Node and Pluto, and these three in combination are the main signature of adult cancer. Childhood cancer seems to follow different rules. Fixed signs are always prominent, and Taurus-Scorpio is stressed in those who have malignancies of the sexual organs. Again we see the theme of thwarted femininity.

Algol is the Great Mother. She is Kali, the Destructive aspect of the White Goddess. Those who have Algol with the Sun have to come to confrontation with the Destroyer and slay her, or they will be turned to stone. Those who triumph over her and cut off her head will mount on Pegasus to greater heights. She was turned to stone.

FLO

43N 39
70W 16

Born May 19, 1912;
11.38 a.m. E.S.T.
(from family Bible.)

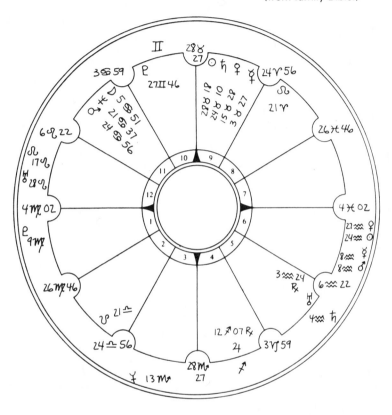

Topocentric

Declinations
Sun 19N48
Moon 28N 18
Mercury 9N 43
Venus 15N 26
Mars 22N 40
Jupiter 21S 28
Saturn 16N 57
Uranus 19S 58
Neptune 21N 11
Pluto 17N 19

An Impeccable Warrior

Carlos Casteneda's Don Juan Matos holds that the impeccable warrior always carries with him the certain knowledge of his own death.

Cancer can be a psychosomatic disease, there is not much doubt about that. It has been linked with an inability to express emotion, and a turning inwards of hostility against oneself.

Although malignant disease is a great mystery, the prevailing theory is that it is triggered by viruses, exposure to radiation, injury, poisons, or mutation, but the underlying cause is a breakdown of the resistance of the body and the inability of the immunological defences to overcome it.

There are many reports of cancer regressing without medical treatment, or with inadequate treatment. It has been postulated that the mind can heal, as well as kill. The interest of this case lies in the fact that it may be one of them.

Carol and Luke were not happily married. It was remarkable that she had finally got married at the age of 31, for she seemed to be afraid of forming close attachments to anyone. Her father died when she was four, and her childhood was financially deprived, as her mother had to work to support the two children. There could not have been much time for the affection and care a mother is supposed to provide, it is probable that Carol has missed this all her life.

Her children were her whole world, but now they are all grown and have left home. She has no friends, and no hobbies.

She has had to live with the knowledge that she had a very malignant type of cancer, which, although it was removed, can recur at any time.

In our present state of evolution, the hardest lessons are those which are concerned with getting on with other people.

The most important houses of the chart to consider for this are the seventh, eighth, fifth and fourth. The seventh is the house of close relationships, such as marriage, the fifth is our creativity and loves, and the fourth is the home, the shelter and refuge into which we can withdraw. The eighth indicates the power struggle for dominance in a marriage, and how resources will be used. It often works in the sphere of money and sex.

Probably Leo is one of the worst signs to have on the Ascendant if one desires a happy marriage. Aquarius then falls on the seventh cusp, and the partner chosen is likely to show the humanitarian characteristics of Aquarius, who has a conscience about the needs of society but is liable to be neglectful of his nearest and dearest. Aquarius has little sense of personal attachment. This does not suit Leo, who needs to be in the limelight, and if this is impossible, may withdraw from life as Carol did.

Scorpio is on the fourth cusp. This is a proud, secretive, and brooding sign. She lavished her passion on her children, but could not rule her husband, who eluded her grasp.

Sagittarius is on the fifth cusp. Her joy and delight is found in travelling. Sagittarius is often impersonal, and is more apt to think what others can do for him than the other way around.

Pisces is on the eighth cusp, and its ruler Neptune is placed in the twelfth house, where it has a powerful effect on the subconscious mind. I consider this to be one of the prinicipal psychological causes of her illness.

Her husband did not fare much better in his personal relationships, for his seventh house cusp is Aries, which is impatient, egotistical and not at all perceptive of the needs of others, so this is how the woman he chooses will appear to him.

His fifth house sign is Aquarius, and his fourth house sign Capricorn, so the marriage was not one of great warmth and communication.

The chart shows the problems of the life. Carol has a square between the Moon in Taurus in the tenth house and Neptune in Leo in the twelfth. Taurus is a sign for whom the family is very important, and the square to Neptune brought disappointments in her family relationships. She has an opposition, the two old enemies Saturn and Uranus oppose each other form the first to the seventh houses. Uranus wants to have complete freedom, and in marriage one must always compromise, which Carol was not willing to do. Saturn restricted her. The trine between Pluto and Uranus gave her the determination to break away. The climax came when she ran away, taking with her the children, who were nine, seven and five years old. Luke was forced to support her in a separate residence for years. He drove two hundred and sixty miles to see them every weekend. The situation suited her well, because she no longer had to live with him and try unsuccessfully to make him notice her.

The cancer might never have developed had she not been forced back to live with him when she broke her leg in an automobile accident. Uranus at that time was transiting 22 Virgo, in square to her Sun. She had to face the problems in her marriage, no matter how rebellious she felt.

Things did not improve at home, and Carol finally left again, after making Luke sign a separation agreement. A year later, after he had become reconciled to her permanent absence, a malignant melanoma developed in the old scar left from the operation on the leg after the automobile accident. Saturn was transiting in 22 Gemini conjunct her Sun, and she was again forced to return home to Luke so that he could look after her. An extensive operation which removed part of the underlying muscle of the leg had to be carried out.

Melanoma is one of the types of cancer which is increasing in incidence. A recent article in the *Lancet* discussed the cause for the approximately six fold increase in the last ten years. We are in a period of increasing sunspot activity. There is a regular eleven year sun spot cycle, in which the number is at its maximum and then falls off, but the number during the maximum has been very high recently. The radiation which is poured out disrupts the ozone layer and allows more of the ultraviolet light, which is thought to trigger melanoma, to reach the surface of the planet. In melanoma, the skin melanocytes, which carry pigment, become wild and start growing in an irregular and unrestrained manner. Cells break away and are carried to the brain or the lungs, and the patient usually dies quite quickly. Sometimes, however, the *T* cells of the thymus are activated strongly and destroy all the melanin in the body, including the cells of the malignant melanoma. When this happens, a spontaneous cure results.

Speaking astrologically, no one has been able to discover the 'signature' for malignant disease. The Moon has a great deal to do with it, and is often in a fixed sign and configured with Neptune. The outer planets, particularly Pluto, are usually implicated, and may represent the testing we go through as we face death.

The most common configuration is that Saturn is found at the midpoint of the Moons Node and Pluto. Variations may occur, for the midpoint may be in square or semisquare to Saturn, or the Node-Saturn midpoint may be in conjunction, square or semisquare to Pluto. The secondary progressions, where one day after birth is equivalent to one year of life, show progressed Saturn at 10 Virgo, the North Node-Pluto midpoint.

The Sun is the Ascendant ruler, representing the vitality of the body, and had progressed to the midpoint of Jupiter and Neptune when the melanoma was diagnosed. Both these planets detoxify the body, and both occupy the twelfth house natally, indicating the possibility of disease due to their malfunction at some time of the life. The Moon is square Neptune, and rules the lymph system, an important method of spread of cancer.

The twelfth house cusp is Cancer 18, the degree held by Pluto at the time the first atom bomb was dropped. It is a degree associated with destructive energy.

Theories about psychological precursors of cancer relate it to hopelessness, helplessness, denial, repression of negative emotions, particularly anger, and to an inability to cope successfully with a severe emotional loss. Recent evidence from research with biofeedback and behavior modification has shown how the mind can influence the body. Carl Simonton in Texas is working with a form of therapy known as imagery, in which the cancer patient is encouraged to visualise and draw pictures of the cancer in the body. Relaxation exercises are taught, and the patient learns ways of overcoming old angers and resentment. Simonton, a radiologist, claims that many cancers regress under imagery.

The marriage is mended. The possibility of Carol's death drew them closer together. Luke has ceased to think of remarriage, and they live together all winter. When Spring comes, she leaves him and goes to the country home, where he visits her weekends. Her cancer was not properly treated, for it was not operated on for some months after discovery, and she had no chemotherapy. A metastasis in the lymph glands was removed a year after the original operation, but it has not recurred.

My own feeling is that the worst aspects have passed. The progressed Sun will soon emerge from the twelfth house to the Ascendant. An important change may await her when Saturn and Jupiter both transit Libra 8 in 1981. Her husband has his Sun in this degree, and it is the midpoint of her Moon and Uranus, and was on the midheaven by progression when she married. One should never predict death, but there may be the ending of a relationship. Every death has different aspects; for some, it may be a joyous event. Who knows to what we will awaken in the other world?

CAROL

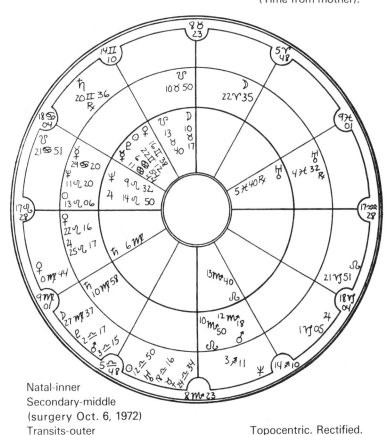

40N 43
74W

Born June 13, 1920;
10 a.m. E.D.S.T.
(Time from mother).

Natal-inner
Secondary-middle
(surgery Oct. 6, 1972)
Transits-outer

Topocentric. Rectified.

Declinations
Sun 23 N 13
Moon 15 N 18
Mercury 24 N 57
Venus 22 N 36
Mars 9 S 11
Jupiter 17 N 11
Saturn 11N 01
Uranus 10 S 09
Neptune 17 N 53
Pluto 19 N 39

A Lonesome Road

Like one who on a lonesome road
Walks on, nor turns his head,
Because he knows a fearful fiend
May close behind him tread.

Mary had a horse. This is all I remember about her childhood. She had a horse and seven brothers, and was greatly envied for both. No one was ever invited to their big house to play, because her mother was 'nervous' and had enough children of her own to look after. They were devout Catholics, and their friends were from the Church, not the community. It was said that the children were not allowed in the living room, and that there were plastic covers on the furniture to keep it clean.

The Neptune in Libra/Uranus in Cancer generation seemed peculiarly unfit for the workaday world. When Venus was involved, they often got into trouble with drugs. I was first called to the house to see Mary in July 1970. She had eaten nothing but brown rice and one glass of water daily for eight days. Her urine was loaded with pus cells, and she was dizzy when she got out of bed. She had recently become engaged, and her husband-to-be was a vegetarian and a macrobiotic diet enthusiast. I warned Mary. Pluto was transiting her Sun in Virgo in the sixth house, she had just graduated from high school and was beginning to feel the pressures of Society. It was no time to play games with her health.

She married and crossed the country to California, where they worked in a vegetarian restaurant. Things were tough, and in January 1972 when she became pregnant, she returned to Maine. Uranus had reached her Moon-Saturn conjunction in April 1972 when her favorite brother hanged himself in the woods, leaving a two year old son and a two week old daughter. I saw Mary at the wake. She is a very beautiful girl, but looked haggard and drawn. Later she said she had "completely flipped out" during her pregnancy. The hallucinations came during the day, and the frightening dreams at night. Devils were all around her. She felt they were following her. Psychiatric counselling did not seem to help. Her obstetrician urged her to eat more for the sake of her unborn child. She was living mostly on rice.

Tina was born in October, 1972. Her husband was very supportive, but Mary did not want to be left with the baby because she could not stand the crying and feared that she would kill the child. In June 1974, she had a uterine suspension and her tubes were tied. The psychiatric counselling continued, and she left her husband and returned home to her parents. Now she was afraid that she would kill herself, and the Valium that was prescribed only made her more depressed. Severe headaches and blackout spells due to hypoglycemia were added to her other symptoms, and she was told that she had to eat eight meals every day.

Hypoglycemia indicates a disorder of insulin production and soon leads to diabetes when the pancreas becomes exhausted. It is indicated by afflictions between Jupiter and Venus, which are here the rulers of the eighth and seventh houses. Note the close conjunction of four planets in Libra quincunx Jupiter. One often sees this kind of configuration in alcoholics, but Virgo is not a sign prone to this disorder, being much too careful of the body. It is also seen in hypoglycemia.

Six planets in the sixth and one in the eighth did not give one much hope that she will ever be entirely healthy. Mars is parallel Pluto and Uranus. This configuration gives deep-seated trouble with coming to terms with one's femininity, as indeed one might guess would be the case with one who had seven brothers and a neurotic mother with a history of trouble in her own generative organs.

I did not see much of Mary during 1974, but in 1975 I

gave her a course of acupuncture treatment and this helped her to relax and sleep better. She had dyspareunia and ovarian pain intermittently, and her marriage finally came to an end. She put her daughter in a day care center, and started a course in recreation direction at a local college so that she could earn a living as a playground director.

Saturn was now in her fifth house approaching her sixth cusp. Neptune is close to her eighth house Mars. A Neptune-Mars configuration often means surgery, especially when it is in the eighth house. In May, Mary underwent fairly major surgery in her ovaries and tubes. A right ovarian cyst was discovered and there were adhesions from the former operation when her tubes were tied. Both tubes were thickened and had been infected at some time by pelvic inflammatory disease. Both were taken, and the right ovary was also removed. The adhesions were lysed.

Since her Moon and Venus were both afflicted, and an afflicted Pluto presided over the fifth house, which also held the South Node, Mary was lucky to have one child. She does not feel that she is sane enough to have more, and the devils are still lurking. I expect that the eclipses in 9 Taurus brought matters to a head, and that when Neptune separates from Mars, she will be able to think more rationally. Meanwhile, it would not surprise me if she had another psychiatric break. The ruler of the twelfth conjunct the ruler of the Ascendant often indicates something of the kind.

It is fortunate that most of the planets are in cardinal signs, because it is much easier to cope with cardinal than with fixed or mutable afflictions. There is more will to face what must be faced, such as surgery, and less of the malaise and nervousness associated with the mutable signs. The fixed signs seem to indicate diseases which cannot be cured. The transits outside the natal chart are the planets at the time of the last operation in May 1977. The secondary positions are in the middle ring.

I have always liked Mary, because she is not prone to self-pity. She is a charming girl, with a difficult chart, and she is doing as best she can. I fear she will have a lonesome road.

MARY

43N 39
70W 16

Born Sept. 20, 1952;
7:45 p.m. E.D.S.T.
(from hospital record).

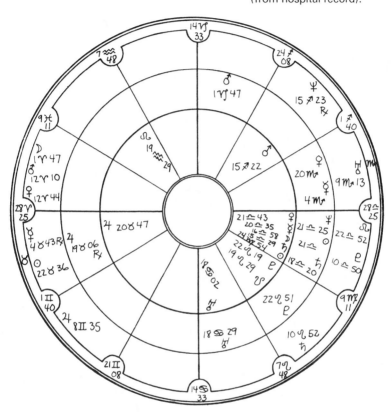

Surgery at 12.55 p.m. May 13, 1977
E.D.S.T., 43N 39, 70W 16:

Transits outer ring, secondary
progression middle ring.

Topocentric.

SUMMARY (Chart XII)

Hypoglycemia.

Venus quincunx Jupiter in a sign of Venus.

Ovarian Cysts. Gyn. Surgery.

Pluto conj. S. Node in 5th square Jupiter., ruler of 8th.

Afflicted Moon (conj. Saturn) and Venus (conj. Neptune.)

Depression and anxiety neurosis-almost certainly with a sexual basis.

Mercury ruler of 6th also rules 3 and Jupiter rules 9.

Many planets in the 6th in Virgo, whose true ruler or at any rate co-ruler is Vesta. Virgo represents the forsaken or neglected child.

The 'starvation' axis Moon-Saturn also occupies the 6th.

A Far, Far Better Thing

The skeins of our lives are so interwoven that we are not always able to identify the time when someone else puts our fortunes on an entirely different track. This is the story of a little boy and how his life was saved by a friend.

It is hard to see in this chart that life was terribly endangered in the early years. Neither are there any obviously dreadful afflictions such as might show cruel and neglectful parents. The fourth house, the domain of childhood, origin, family, and roots, contains no malefic. Venus, the ruler, is trine Pluto and the Moon. It is true that Jupiter, close to Venus, is square the fourth cusp. Does this show an excess of the treatment he received? The ordinary astrologer would judge that his childhood might be lonely, and that his mother might be dominating and unusual, but I do not think that there is any indication of the almost fatal danger he was exposed to, or of the strange manner in which he was saved. Not, at any rate, if only conventional aspects are used.

Billy was the sixth child born to his mother, who was thirty-seven years old and had been previously married. The three elder children had a different father. One of them was killed in an automobile accident before Billy was born; the others lived with her. Billy's father had also been married before. In fact, he had been married twice, and had two grown boys in Texas and two young daughters in Connecticut. He had deserted his second family, but finally the law caught up with him. After doing some time in jail for non-support, he reluctantly decided that he had better send them some money. This left his third family extremely poor. He never earned much, drank heavily, abused his wife, and terrorized the neighborhood. It was well known that he had a gun, and it was clear that he knew how to use it. He unhesitatingly shot his daughter's dog after receiving a complaint about it. After this, none of the neighbors dared cross him in any way.

Billy was born on December 17, 1973 at 8:39 a.m. in Portland, Maine, and I looked after him for a time when he was an infant. He seemed a healthy child, well nourished at the age of six months, weighing eighteen pounds. As his birth weight was seven pounds five ounces, there was no evidence that anything was amiss. I heard later that his mother had a strange belief that he was her child who had been killed in the automobile accident and who had come back to her. He was a very winning little boy, he had Venus rising and Moon in Libra and all the charm that went with them. His mother became afraid that she would lose him in an accident if she took him out, and some time after I last saw him, she began to keep him in his room. The other children went to school, but he was left at home. He was never let out. Sometimes his youngest brother threw beanbags and toys at him, and he was covered with bruises. He did not learn to walk very well, because he was not encouraged to get out of his crib. He seemed forlorn and forgotten. His only friend was his young uncle Leon, who doted on him. This was extremely strange, because Leon was generally regarded as a no good bum, a delinquent, and always in trouble with the authorities. Every Saturday he came to the house to take Billy out. He bathed him, dressed him in clean clothes, and took him out to eat.

The neighbors had a very good idea of how things were in the household, but no one said anything, since they were afraid of the violent temper and the gun of Billy's father.

Leon worried a good deal about Billy. His sister wanted to adopt him, for she was childless, but in spite of the poverty of the family, they would not hear of it.

In 1976 there was a general tightening up of eligibility for food stamps, and Billy's family was told that they were no longer eligible. Matters went from bad to worse. It seemed that Billy was not getting enough to eat, and he became thinner and did not look at all healthy. Leon became more worried.

At Christmas, the other children attended their school parties, played with their toys, and went visiting in the neighborhood. Billy was not allowed out of his room, and this enraged Leon and he brooded about it. Finally the outbreak came on January 30 at 3 a.m., when Leon broke down the door of the house, picked Billy up, and charged down to the police station with him, shouting, "This is a case of child abuse. Do something!" The police had Billy admitted to the children's ward of the hospital, and he was found to be close to death from starvation.

It is hard to believe, but this three year old child, who had weighed eighteen pounds at six months, now weighed nineteen pounds. His hair was very thin and sparse. He was very small, and tottered as he walked, from weakness due to disuse of his muscles. He had a bone age of eighteen months. Curiously enough, he was friendly and out going, and chattered away to anyone who would listen. He seemed to crave company. A special volunteer was given to him, for the sole purpose of providing tender loving care. He was fed, and gained five pounds in two weeks. At the end of this time, he was placed in a foster home where he is living happily at the present time. His family misses him, and his mother has tried hard to get him back. The judge, however, having considered the evidence, has decided that his home is not safe for him, and he will never be allowed to live there again. The foster parents have applied to adopt him, and it seems their request will be granted.

How do we read this chart? Starvation is usually shown by afflictions to Saturn and the Moon, for it comes under the 4-10 axis. If starvation had occured after childhood, I would expect the actual rulers of the fourth and tenth houses to be involved. Cruelty from the parents is shown by an afflicted Moon and Saturn.

The Moon is afflicted by its conjunction with Pluto, and they are in the eighth house. This is a very poor placement for the Moon, unless well aspected. It often occurs in children who die before their seventh birthday. The eighth house is ruled by Mercury, which is quincunx the fourth cusp. Note that Pluto is approaching a quincunx to the fourth cusp from the opposite side of the midheaven.

It may not seem that Saturn is severely afflicted, except by the square to the Moon and Pluto. However, there is a powerful aspect to Mars, a paran. Cyril Fagan and Rob Hand have both written about parans. Although there may be no zodiacal aspect, planets on simultaneous angles reinforce each other in the fourth harmonic. When Capricorn 1° 44' is on the Ascendant, and natal Saturn on the seventh cusp, in Portland, Maine, 43 N 39 latitude, 28 Aries, the degree holding natal Mars, will be on the fourth cusp. Saturn is therefore paran square Mars. This is a powerful aspect and signifies that the native will receive brutal treatment from those who are represented by Mars. The tenth house, that of the dominant parent, is ruled by Mars and Pluto.

Why did this child behave as he did? For one thing, he has no planets in Earth, and for another, the North Node in the twelfth house often indicates someone who gets less than he deserves. Saturn is his Ascendant ruler. How does he see himself—for this is what the Ascendant signifies. How does he think he should behave? Saturn retrograde tells you what not to do. It is in the sixth house, a house of mind. Does this mean that he sees himself as a slave, powerless and expecting nothing? Is this why he allowed himself to be starved? Is it because a cadent house placement ensures that there will be non-expression by violent means of the ego?

The child who has this placement will suffer in silence. If Saturn had been angular, he would not have allowed himself to be confined in his room without sufficient food to eat, but would have rebelled. Instead, he turned the energy inward and inflicted punishment on himself. Saturn retrograde shows a masochistic nature. Saturn in the sixth house shows heavy discipline during childhood. The Moon disposes of Saturn and is in close conjunction with Pluto in the eighth house, which is in itself an indication of masochism. One might suspect from this that the mother would be the instrument through whom the tendency to self-punishment would be brought about.

BILLY

43N 39
70W 16

Born on Dec. 17, 1973;
8.39 a.m. E.S.T.
(from hospital record).

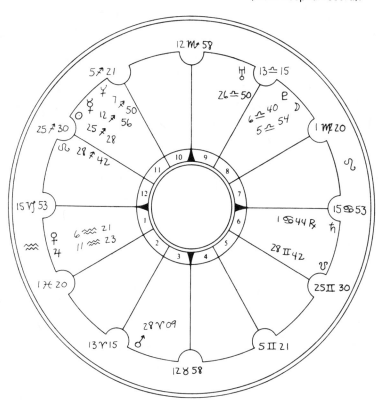

Declinations
Sun 23S 21
Moon 4S 34
Mercury 22S 03
Venus 20S 07
Mars 11N 30
Jupiter 18S 06
Saturn 22N 22
Neptune 20S 05
Uranus 9S 48
Pluto 12N 28

Topocentric.

Venus and Jupiter rising give him a charming nature, eager to please, and the stellium in the eleventh house reinforces this.

In March 1977, when Billy was placed in foster care by the Court, Pluto was retrograding through the fourteenth degree of Libra, forming the double quincunx or Yod to the fourth cusp, together with natal Mercury. The North Node was transiting across the natal Uranus, releasing the energy of the Mars-Uranus opposition.

It is interesting to look at the chart of his young uncle, born on October 15, 1957. Jupiter conjuncts Mars in 14 Libra, and the transit of Pluto over this degree no doubt brought about the explosion which swept Billy away to a new life. His uncle Leon still visits him every week and takes him out to dinner. He reports that Billy is happy, thriving, and has almost forgotten that he once had another family.

Playing God

It was with great pity and a sense of guilt that I studied the record: "The woman was an obese eighteen year old, dull looking, but seeming to understand. She was in a wheelchair. The chief complaint is of fecal incontinence secondary to her long previous history of paraplegia. She enters hospital to have a colostomy."

Gayle was born with a meningomyelocele. The lower end of the spinal cord, from which arise the nerves supplying the bladder, bowel and legs, was exposed in a sac, and covered only with a thin layer of skin. (Neural tube defects can now be diagnosed in pregnancy by a blood test on the mother, and by a test of the amniotic fluid.)

In the old days, the sac always began to leak spinal fluid and became infected. Then the child died of meningitis.

About twenty years ago, surgery had become sufficiently advanced to be able to operate on these children. The nerves in the sac can be freed and covered with skin. The children then lived, because they did not become infected, but even the most 'successful' cases developed hydrocephalus and mental retardation.

When Gayle was born, this complication was well recognized, and to prevent it, a shunt was constructed to take away excess fluid from the ventricles of the brain. In her case, the left kidney was removed and the shunt placed in the left ureter.

The technique has improved, and now it is placed in the atrium of the heart. The excess fluid passes into the circulation. There is little risk in the procedure although some cases have developed pulmonary hypertension, which is fatal! However, Gayle was born before this method was introduced. Her developing hydrocephalus was arrested, and though a "slow learner," she definitely was not retarded. She seemed a normal nine year old, although desperately ill when she entered hospital with *E. coli meningitis*, which had then reached the brain from a urinary tract infection on November 17, 1967.

It seemed that she would probably die. Meningitis alone is a potentially fatal disease, but meningitis in the presence of a brain to ureter shunt is impossible to cure without removing the shunt, which acts as a foreign body. Antibiotic treatment began at once, but despite this, the pressure in the brain was very great and kept increasing. The blood pressure rose with it, in order to maintain the flow of blood through the brain. It reached the incredible height of 300/200, and we had called in a neurosurgeon to put a pressure monitor in her skull when she suddenly herniated her brainstem through the *foramen magnum* and sank into a very deep coma. She was totally paralyzed, both arms and legs, and death seemed but hours away.

It was the weekend, I was on duty and sat with her. She was bleeding into her stomach and into her skin, lungs, and brain. Unless the blood pressure could be reduced, she would bleed to death. I started mannitol, cortisone, thorazine, reserpine, but none brought it down. As a last resort, I put up an Arfonad drip, a ganglionie blocking agent to dilate the blood vessels which were in spasm and keeping her pressure so high. She was very insensitive to it, but I sat with her through the night and monitored her. Little by little the bleeding ceased and so she lived.

I never thought she would be paralyzed. Her arms gradually returned to normal, but her legs never moved again.

After her blood pressure and intracranial pressure had stabilized, and her kidney function, which temporarily had ceased, returned, she was taken to the operating room and the shunt was removed. The meningitis slowly cleared.

I do not know how much her brain was damaged, and whether it was due to the meningitis or the high pressure. She seemed much more retarded after her illness. Her family could not cope with looking after her in a wheel chair, and she was sent to an institution for retarded children where she remained for several years.

The legs used to go into intolerably painful muscle spasms. A cordotomy was done, an operation to cut the nerves in the spinal cord. She was incontinent of urine, so her bladder was removed and her ureters diverted into the bowel. Then she was incontinent of faeces, so a colostomy was carried out in April 1977.

She had had a nervous breakdown and was in the psych ward in the summer of 1976. She must have insight into her condition, for people who are very retarded do not have acute psychotic episodes.

I have seen her once since then. She was in a wheelchair, and she did not remember her illness. Since then, she has seen more doctors than one can count, and her treatment must have run into thousands of dollars. Worse than that is the thought as to the kind of future she has to look forward to.

So much for playing God.

GAYLE

43N 39
70W 16

July, 14, 1968;
10.32 p.m. E.D.S.T.
(Hospital record).

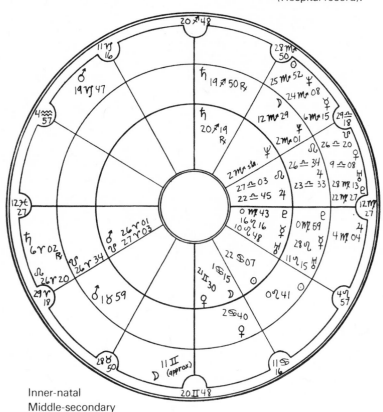

Inner-natal
Middle-secondary
Outer-transits for Nov. 18, 1967.

Topocentric.

Declinations.
Sun 21N 38
Moon 18N 55
Mercury 16N 48
Venus 22N 01
Mars 7N 49
Jupiter 7N 43
Saturn 21S 44
Uranus 18N 10
Neptuen 10S 31
Pluto 21N 52

SYNOPSIS

Natally, there are two striking configurations:

1. The *T* square between Mars in 26 Aries with the South Node, the Sun in 22 Cancer, and Jupiter in 22 Libra.

Mars is one of the rulers of the first house, and Neptune, placed in the eighth house, is the other. Mars in the first house indicates that the brain, or the head which contains it, is liable to be affected if Mars is in aspect to the sixth house ruler, in this chart the Sun.

At the time of surgery, on November 22, 1967, Mars was in 22 Capricorn making a Grand Cross and opposing the natal Sun.

2. The Saturn-Venus opposition across the M.C.-I.C. axis, in mundane square to the Ascendant.

At the time of her near fatal illness, the progressed chart had a very similar configuration. Mars was in square to the Sun and opposition Neptune. Death seemed almost certain, but Venus, one of the rulers of the eighth house, was in 2 Cancer sextile Mars, and Pluto, the other eighth house ruler, was in Virgo in trine to mars and sextile Neptune.

The secondary *T* square afflicted the axis of the 2-8, giving renal shutdown and problems of electrolyte imbalance, and also circulatory problems since the 11th house is the empty arm of the *T* Mars, being involved, brings that which is signified by natal Mars into manifestation.

The declinations have a much more physical effect than aspects in the Zodiac. The natal Sun is parallel Pluto, Venus and Saturn, the Nodes are parallel Neptune, and transiting Jupiter was parallel the Nodes and Neptune on the day of the operation, November 22.

These heavy afflictions to the ruler of the sixth have made her life dependent on the resources of Society. Pisces is not considered a fortunate sign when on the Ascendant, and one wonders how much more she will have to endure before she is released from the burden of life.

Like a Butterfly

Dale was retarded. It is impossible to diagnose his retardation from his chart by using the classical astrological methods. A great many excellent astrologers tried, because he was one of the retarded children who was paired with gifted children in the test given by the National Council of Geocosmic Research.

There is a stellium of planets in Dale's sixth house, which in my system of diagnosis indicates a disorder present from birth. The ruler of the twelfth, Mercury, is among them indicating that the disorder is a serious one and will imprison him in some way. If one uses the asteroids, the stellium is increased in influence, for Pallas, Vesta, and Juno are all in Sagittarius in the sixth house.

The strong emphasis on the sixth house bears out the remark made to me by an astrologer that Virgo is the deserted child. The Moon from the Midheaven squares these sixth house planets from Pisces, the natural ruler of the twelfth house, adding further emphasis to this area. The Moon is doubly important, for not only is she the Ascendant ruler, but also the planet most important in childhood. Sirius rises in conjunction with the North Node. Neptune, the ruler of Pisces, is afflicted by the square of Saturn from the eighth house, and Mercury is afflicted by the square of Uranus. One would consider his chart to pose a difficult life's task, but one that would be successfully surmounted because most of the afflictions are in mutable signs. As things turned out, this was probably correct if one takes a cosmic point of view. He did not live long, but his life was not unhappy and gave an opportunity for unselfish service to those who looked after him.

I always had the feeling that Dale was imprisoned. His body was grotesque, but sometimes a fleeting smile lit up his whole face. Probable I was just responding to his foster mother's absolute devotion; and yet there are many retarded children for whom one can feel nothing, because they hardly seem to belong to the human race.

He brought happiness to those who looked after him for nine years, and it was wonderful that he found a family so devoted to him. He was the most retarded child I have ever seen. His brain damage was so extensive that he grew to a weight of fifteen pounds and then stopped growing, so he always looked like a baby.

His mother had eight children, and when Dale was being born, the placenta separated prematurely. After extreme blood loss, a badly shocked and apparently lifeless infant was delivered. He was resuscitated, as no one can tell for sure how much, if any, brain damage there will be, since the brain of the newborn infant is very resistant to lack of oxygen. However, it soon became apparent that the damage had been very severe.

His mother refused to look after him, and the State took him into custody. A very loving and caring foster mother was found, and Dale was looked after for the rest of his life as if he were the most precious thing in the world. In truth, the lives of his foster mother, foster father, and foster sister revolved around him. No child could have had better care.

It was impossible to know if Dale even recognized his foster parents. He did not focus his eyes properly, had no head control, and spent his life propped up in a wheel chair. His family thought that he enjoyed television, particularly the cartoons, and his eyes followed the screen as if with some understanding. He had to be fed, bathed, and diapered as if he were four months old. I saw him twice a year for physical checkups, and he never had any medical problems except for excessive amounts of mucus secretions which he could not cough up. His family never gave up hope that one day he would begin to grow and his brain would develop.

The end came unexpectedly. A day care center for the retarded was opened, and Dale attended it to have his limbs massaged and put through a range of movement by a physical therapist. It was also thought that he might enjoy being taken out with the other children to the playground in his wheelchair. No one knew how it happened, but one day he managed to jam his hand behind a radiator, and before it could be freed, he had a bad burn. I saw him and cleansed it and applied a dressing of sterile Furacin gauze, the standard treatment for burns. He was malnourished in spite of an excellent diet, and the burn did not heal. Finally, it became infected. I suspected *pseudomonas septicemia*, and admitted him to hospital for treatment. The house staff were incredulous that such a poor wizened little thing should be of such value to his family, and it was pointed out to me that antibiotic treatment for pseudomonas would cost about two hundred dollars a day. "Nevertheless," I insisted, "I want no effort spared to keep him alive." It was in vain. About thirty hours after admission, on March 24, 1973, he stopped breathing. The autopsy showed a brain which had almost entirely been replaced by fibrous tissue, like that of a very old man.

His family grieved for him, but they were thankful that he had brought them happiness for nine years. They were well known in the small Maine community in which they lived, and Dale was given a memorial service which half the town attended. His fifteen year old sister wrote a special poem for him which began,

How wonderful for Dale
Free at last, he burst out like a butterfly
Rises from his ugly prison.

DALE

43N 39
70W 16

Born Nov. 25, 1963;
6.47 p.m. E.S.T.
(Hospital record).

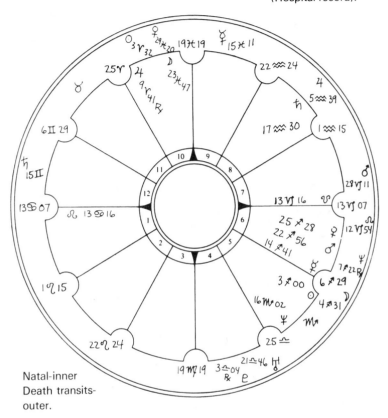

Natal-inner
Death transits-
outer.

Topocentric.

Declinations
Sun 20S 46
Moon 6S 56
Mercury 24S 24
Venus 24S 25
Mars 24S 06
Jupiter 2N 28
Saturn 16S 43
Uranus 8N 36
Neptune 14S 58
Pluto 18N 50

Knowledge is Power

This case shows that nothing is hopeless, no matter how bad the aspects may be. If one takes things into one's own hands early enough, victory can be won from apparent defeat.

I do not think that any astrologer would have given much for the chances of survival from a malignancy discovered when Pluto, Saturn, and the Sun were in a close Yod formation, which involved the progressed Ascendant, natal eighth cusp, and was also threatened by a South Node eclipse ten months later on April 29, 1976.

However, the native was himself a physician. Whitney discovered a thickening in his right testicle, realized what it meant and at once sought surgical advice. His roommate at college, curiously enough, had developed the same malignancy. It was only in Stage 1, which meant that the lymph nodes draining the site were uninvolved. He had two immediate operations; an orchidectomy to remove the embryonal seminoma, and a pelvic lymph gland removal to stage it. Although the five year period for clinical cure has not yet gone by, and he has some very bad aspects coming up, his physicians were sure that there was no danger of a recurrance. The outlook for a Stage 1 embryonal seminoma is excellent.

Although one does not now talk about good and bad charts, it is easy to see that his natal chart has every planet afflicted except Mercury, and Mercury is in the sixth house, considered a weak and not altogether fortunate position.

He will have a difficult life, you will say, and his salvation will be through Mercury and how he pays his debt to Society.

If he works very hard serving his fellow man, Whitney will find contentment and have the satisfaction of a job well done.

The outer planets during the 1940's form many hard aspects to the inner planets, and this is appropriate for a generation born during a world war.

The Sun here is conjunct Saturn and square Pluto. Traditionally, this shows trouble with the father. Here not only is there rejection and coldness due to the Sun-Saturn contact, but there is actual danger of violence due to the affliction by Pluto. In this case, his father used to fly into rages and beat him severely. He must have felt it necessary to prove his worth, and he was successful in this, for his academic achievements are impressive. Whitney has succeeded in carving out a career and living a seemingly normal life with a wife and child. It could not have been easy, and it required the tenacity and will to survive which is the great gift of Taurus.

The Moon is in a loose *Yod* formation with Jupiter and Neptune. He tells me that his mother was psychologically abnormal, depressed, and did not want any children. He is an only child, and was never accepted by her. Note that the Moon is in Scorpio, the sign of her fall, and void-of-course.

The opposition, fortunately not close, between Moon and Uranus must have played a role in moulding his sexuality, since the houses involved are the second and eighth. Indeed, the second and eighth houses and signs are stressed above all, and it is not hard to guess that if he ever developed a malignancy, it would be one arising in the reproductive organs.

The Sun-Saturn contact makes him very hard working and serious. He has qualifications in both internal medicine and psychiatry, and one gets the impression that he feels guilty when he is not working. He must have a deep inner need for self denial. It is fortunate that he was blessed with a Libra Ascendant, for this lends a lightness of touch, otherwise sadly lacking.

The Mc/Asc. midpoint is 28 Leo, in close square to his afflicted Moon. His mother has had more of an influence on him than he recognizes.

Malignant disease appears to be a fixed sign affliction, and the Moon rather that the Sun is usually in a fixed sign. In this chart, Moon and Sun, both afflicted by outer planets, are in fixed signs, and the emphasis of the chart, by the counting of triplicities and quadruplicities, is fixed earth.

On February 28, 1975 his cancer was discovered. The secondary aspects and the transits pick out the eighth cusp very exactly. Yet he did not die. He then must have suffered a severe shock which caused him to restructure his life. Uranus has recently passed in opposition to his natal Sun-Saturn conjunction, and he said that this was when he decided to be his own man. He had been trying to find himself, as the phrase goes, and thought he had finally succeeded.

Although natal Mercury is unafflicted, it was strongly affected by the transit of Pluto directly in opposition. Any sixth house planet, whether afflicied or not, can show a disease. The kind of disease has nothing to do with the natal planet but only with the planet which afflicts it. This is clearly shown here. I believe Pluto to be the main significator of malignant disease. Natally Pluto is parallel Mars.

The *Yod*, or one planet at the apex of a *Y* with two other planets in 150° aspect from it, is said to mean that there is a free choice by the ego, and the matter can go either way. It is connected with illness and with separation, for it is a sixth-eighth house aspect.

Pluto, which is at the apex of the *Y*, is the key planet in the configuration.

It is as if the choice of death or a new beginning and regeneration was offered. The closest aspect to transiting Pluto is natal Mercury, in the sixth house.

Among other things, Mercury rules communication through writing. At the moment, a book is planned, and research for it is being carried out. There are many eclipses in the future which touch off both Mercury and Neptune in the twelfth house. I told him that he would be cut off from Society in some way starting around his next birthday. "That will probably be because I am writing my book," he said. "The research should be all done by then." I must confess that the thought had occurred to me that he might have a recurrence of his cancer. A twelfth house eclipse is often an ominous thing, but not always. In this case, I think the energy has an outlet in the use to which he is putting his Mercury. A sublimation to a higher level is well known in astrology.

The main lesson Whitney has to learn in this life is survival, and the more bad experiences he goes through, the better he will be able to help his patients.

It is interesting to look at his ninth harmonic, which John Addey feels represents the fruits of life.

The transits seem to say that he will be spared to live on. Jupiter is in 2 Scorpio 34, Moon is in 9 Pisces 23, and Pluto is in 5 Aries 40. Transiting Venus, transiting Sun, and transiting Uranus are therefore closely aspected. The ninth harmonic South node is in 25 Virgo 46, and the North Node is therefore conjunct transiting Jupiter. Neptune is in 28 Cancer opposition transiting Mars. Uranus is in 7 Cancer 55 square natal Mercury. These are all very close aspects. Hindu astrologers consider that the ninth harmonic chart overrules the natus, and here it may be significant.

Every truly important event is heralded by an eclipse. On ⟨ October 12, 1977 (19 Libra 29), near the North Node, is the eclipse point and it falls on natal North Node.

On April 7. 1978 the eclipse in 17 Aries 34, more ominous because it is a South Node eclipse, falls 150° from the twelfth cusp. In April 1978, Pluto is in 14 Libra 51 square the M.C.

The lunation on his birthday April 23, 1978 is in 2 Scorpio 43. Mars is in 4 Leo 37 square natal Saturn.

The eclipse of September 16, 1978 is in 23 Pisces 29, closely opposed to Neptune; and the next one, in 8 Libra 48 in October is opposition Mercury.

At the time of the September 16th eclipse, Venus is in 7 Scorpio 50 still within 1 degree of an opposition to progressed Saturn, and Jupiter is in 1 Leo 58.

One hopes that Uranus opposition his natal position will herald the birth of his new book, which is about an eighth house subject.

Postscript

The twelfth house rules hospitals. A twelfth house influence in most people discharges its energy by illness. In the case of a physician there are other ways of discharging the energy, such as working in a hospital.

The eclipse of April 1978 which fell 150° from his twelfth cusp did not signify that he would be admitted to hospital as a patient. Whitney was offered a fine position as the director of the psychiatric services in the largest hospital in the area which was exactly what he had wanted. The energies are expressing themselves on a higher level.

WHITNEY

40N 45
73W57

Born 4.50 p.m.
April 23, 1940.
Information from patient.

R.A.M.C. 105 29.

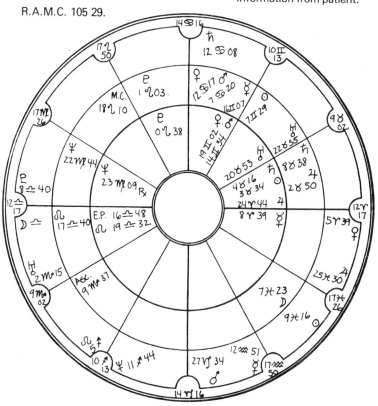

Ca testis diagnosed on Feb. 28, 1975
Natal inner ring
Secondary middle ring
transits outer ring

Topocentric.

The Many Faces of Love

It has been said that character is destiny. Each generation has its own diseases. I predict that Neptune in Scorpio will sow the seeds of liver disease, malignant diseases, and the late consequences of venereal disease. We will see the results when Pluto enters Scorpio in 1984.

Hepatitis B is sexually transmitted, and I suspect that many cases of cirrhosis of the liver, now seen more and more in non-drinkers, will be found to be due to this form of hepatitis contracted years earlier. Carcinoma of the cervix is now thought to be associated with infection by herpes virus type 2, which is also sexually transmitted. It is being seen at an earlier age than ever before. There has already been a great increase in the incidence of both.

Laurie began life under a great handicap. Her young sister died of leukemia four months after she was born. She was pampered and spoiled from that day on, and has never had to do anything which she did not want to do. The thought that she might have some obligation to society or her parents simply never entered her head.

Her family was church-going and extremely respectable, having lived quietly in the community for about six generations. I saw Laurie with stomach pains and arthritis when she was only thirteen, and diagnosed gonorrhea. A few months later, she became pregnant, and gave birth to a son around her fifteenth birthday. He had a club foot. (Note that the Sun rules the fifth house and is in Pisces.)

The young couple were married, and the sixteen year old

husband moved in to live with her family. He was as lazy and self indulgent as Laurie. The care of the baby, as well as the cooking, marketing, laundry and housework, fell on her mother, since Laurie had never helped around the house. After about a year, her husband ran away, and she began dating again almost immediately.

The result was another attack of gonorrhea. This time it was not so easily cured, because it was the resistant South Asian strain, recently introduced into the United States. She was in great pain with spasm of the colon and inflammation of the tubes. It is likely to have made her sterile. Fortunately I was able to cure it with a new antibiotic, for it does not respond to penicillin.

The chart shows Venus, the ruler of the Ascendant, in the twelfth house and detriment in a sign ruled by Mars. Mercury and Venus are the sixth house rulers, and Mercury is opposed by Pluto. One would expect some kind of sexual disorder.

Pluto is the ruler of the seventh house and is placed in the fifth, the house of creativity. The Sun is opposition Pluto, indicating that the man she chooses must have sexual power. Her eighth house is ruled by Jupiter, and since Jupiter is conjunct Saturn, she seeks a father image. Her own father is weak and the eighth house is where other people's power is felt. Pluto is square the cusp, indicating painful sexual experiences and a yielding to the sexual power of the male. Neptune is in the seventh, so she has delusions about her chosen mate. The Jupiter-Saturn conjunction forms the apex of a *Yod*, involving the Moon in the second and Uranus in Leo in the fifth house. Her emotions are easily stirred, but Saturn is the most powerful of the four planets, being in his own sign and house. She must learn self discipline.

The *Yod* formation dominates the chart. According to the rules of medical astrology, when the rulers of the sixth house, Venus and Mercury, are in aspect to it by progression or transit, the illness promised by the natal chart will occur.

It happened that on the day she came to me for her second attack of gonorrhea, as shown in the three ringed chart, that transiting Mercury was with natal Urnanus and transiting Moon with natal Neptune. Venus by secondary progression was square the apex of the Y, the Saturn-Jupiter conjunction. Progressed Pluto was on the exact degree of the North Node, and twenty-five days later she ended her first marriage and entered a new one. The South Node was transiting her natal Venus. This marriage, to a Scorpio man, seems much more likely to last. She has also escaped from the influence of her mother by moving to another town.

The signature of cirrhosis of the liver is a conjunction of Saturn and Jupiter. This is likely to occur when she is in her fifties and most of the planets are in Capricorn.

I saw her recently with scabies. Her husband has a brother who is living with them. He works on the night shift, and her husband works on the day shift, and they all sleep in one bed. They all had scabies, including the baby. Neptune is still influencing her marriage.

The most important event in the life of Laurie was the death of her sister. It is neccessary for her to grow up and live her own life away from the influence of her parents. They love her very much, but their love has proved destructive, and it is fortunate that she has now freed herself.

LAURIE

43N 39
70W 16

Born on Feb. 24, 1961;
8.47 a.m. (Hospital record).

R.A.M.C. 290 12

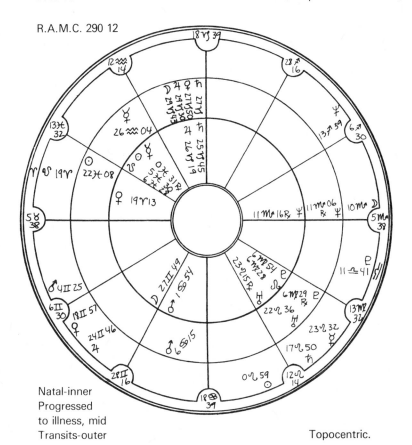

Natal-inner
Progressed
to illness, mid
Transits-outer

Topocentric.

Declinations
Sun 9S 23
Moon 18N 38
Mercury 8S
Venus 11N 06
Mars 26N 33
Jupiter 21S 05
Saturn 20S 57
Uranus 14N 30
Neptune 13S 30
Pluto 21N 07

A Case of Iatrogenic Disease

About twenty-five years ago, it was very fashionable to use X-rays and other radiation treatment for enlarged tonsils and persistent thymus glands because they could easily be shrunk without having to be removed. The fad did not last long. Since the seeds of cancer, when planted, do not grow for about fifteen or twenty years, it was only recently that the realization dawned that carcinoma of the thyroid gland was becoming more common. It was nearly always found in those who had been irradiated. A parallel with the D.E.S. daughters is seen.

It is now thought to be advisable to supervise these irradiated children carefully, since about ten per cent of them will eventually develop tumors of the thyroid gland. I know of two people born in the same month, both irradiated. One actually had a malignant thyroid nodule removed, and the other has a nodule which is cold on scan but not malignant.

The big question is, will it be malignant? One might think that it would be better to have it removed. Instead, the patient's thyroid is being suppressed by a dose of two grains a day of thyroid, which, by an intricate feedback mechanism mediated through the pituitary gland, prevents her own thyroid from producing its hormone.

Here is the chart of a young woman, Mary Lou, who developped a malignancy at the age of twenty-six, and had it removed. She is in good health now, and there is not likely to be a recurrence.

It is possible, however, that Mary Lou some day will have

a different malignancy. Some people are inclined to the unrestrained growth of cells, and some are not. It has been known for six or seven different and unrelated primary cancers to arise over the years in the same patient. It is well known that breast cancer is likely to develop years later in the unaffected side. Perhaps, it will arise in the other breast and usually in a mirror image position. This is what saved Happy Rockefeller's life, since there was no sign of a second tumor, but biopsy of the unaffected side in the mirror image position showed a small positive nodule.

There is no consensus of astrologers about the thyroid gland. Its rulership has been given a Venus (ruler of Taurus, the neck), Neptune (general ruler of glands), Mecury, and Uranus.

Cornell says, "Ruled by Mercury and the signs Taurus and Scorpio. The Moon when in Taurus rules and affects this gland. The thyroid gland acts as a connecting link between the Pineal gland and the Pituitary Body. Neptune afflicted by Saturn, Neptune, or Uranus afflicted in Taurus, all malefics in Taurus, Saturn conjunct Uranus in Taurus." As a physician, I do not agree with this at all.

I have suffered from an overactive thyroid myself, and believe the gland is ruled by Mercury and Uranus. I know of no disease with only one indicator. A disease has a certain signature composed of two or more planets in combination.

The secondary directions and the transits seem to bear me out. The progressed Sun was in a close conjunction with natal Mercury. An eclipse on November 2, eighteen days before surgery, fell in 9 Scorpio 09, just within the allowable one degree orb. Natal and progressed Uranus was quincunx the Ascendant from the eighth, the house of surgery. Transiting Urnaus conjuncted Neptune and transiting Pluto conjuncted the North Node. Transiting Sun was in a very significant position. Of course every year on November 20th, it transits opposite the natal Saturn-Uranus conjunction; but this year, it triggered a very significant experience and brought the whole theme of death and regeneration into her life.

Saturn conjunct Uranus in the eighth house will teach her the meaning of the eighth house: power and psychological insight, the use of her own power to expand her consciousness, the meaning of birth and death, how that which is destroyed will be born again, because it has fulfilled its purpose, the isolation of loneliness and loss, and new beginnings.

Cancer is a great astrological and medical mystery, but it probably has to do with the outer planets and the nodes and especially with Pluto, all of which were activated at this time. Here Pluto is natally parallel the eighth cusp.

This native belongs to an interesting group, the souls who incarnated in the year of the great conjunctions in Taurus in May 1941. Astrologers predicted something spectacular for that year, maybe peace, since Venus rules Taurus. Rudolf Hess, said to have taken astrological advice, stole a plane and flew from Germany to Scotland to offer to turn his country over to Churchill. He spent the rest of his life in prison. This generation has been the most affluent in history. Now the world's resources are running out. Before their lives come to an end, they will have seen the depletion of the oil reserves and a different way of life will come. I think that it is President Carter's karmic mission to develop other energy sources and to set the world on the path it must follow in future times. It would be interesting to know if any of the 1941 generation are on his staff. The emphasis in this chart is on Scorpio and Taurus. The ruler Venus is in Scorpio opposing Urnaus and Saturn, and Jupiter is also in the eighth house. This young woman will need plenty of courage, but Mars in Aries will bring her through it all fighting. At the time of the operation, Saturn was in Aries approaching an opposition to the Sun and forcing her to evaluate her life with the realization that it might be short.

Mary Lou is an ordinary housewife, pleasant and normal, with four children, but one wonders what other eighth house experiences life may have in store for her.

Postscript

The other chart, that of Frances, is somewhat similar. She has the same eighth house conjunction of Saturn and Uranus, and on Nov. 22, 1975, when the Sun was transiting in opposition to this area, her father was killed in an automobile accident.

She visited a famous Hindu astrologer in Delhi and was told that her bones would become decalcified, and that she should eat more foods containing calcium and wear pearls, the jewel of the Moon, to help ameliorate the condition. The parathyroids, which control the calcium balance of the body, are closely adherent to the thyroid, and during operations on the thyroid gland, the parathyroids are often accidently removed or injured.

MARY LOU

44N 02
69W 29

Born on Oct. 6, 1941 E.S.T.
7.12 a.m.
From baby book.

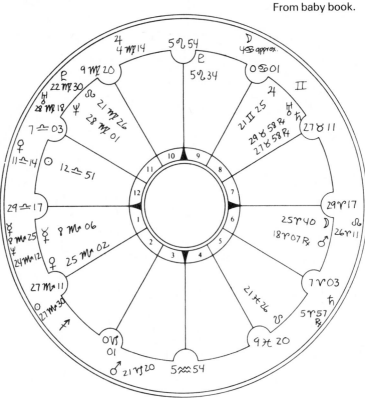

Operated on for thyroid
cancer Nov. 20, 1967.
Transits in outer ring.

Placidus
Calculated by Neil Michelson

Declinations (natal	Declinations (surgery)
Sun 5S 04	Sun 19S 36
Moon 7S 14	Moon 28N 09
Mercury 17S 10	Mercury 12N 11
Venus 20S 43	Venus 2N 55
Mars 3N 45	Mars 23S 13
Jupiter 22N 28	Jupiter 10N 47
Saturn 17N 27	Saturn 0S 02
Uranus 19N 56	Uranus 1N 21
Neptune 1N 57	Neptune 17S 12
Pluto 23N 10	Pluto 16N 38

FRANCES

43N 39
70W 16

Born on Oct. 15, 1941;
5.55 a.m. E.S.T.
From birth certificate.

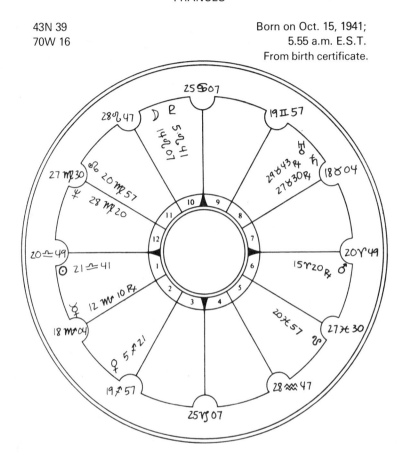

Placidus.
calculated by Neil Michelson.

Declinations
Sun 8 S 28
Moon 13 N 19
Mercury 18 S 36
Venus 23 S 24
Mars 3 N 14
Jupiter 22 N 28
Saturn 17 N 19
Uranus 19 N 53
Neptune 1 N 49
Pluto 23 N 10

Hobson's Choice

This is the story of Mary Elizabeth, born prematurely by Caesarian section at 10:36 p.m. on August 30, 1977. It is said that there is a time to be born and a time to die, and the time she was born turned out to be a very poor choice on the part of her doctors. She had excellent medical care, apart from this factor of time, but the medical considerations led to a birth at a time which was disastrous, not only for Mary Elizabeth, but also for her mother, who will never be able to have another child.

Her mother had high blood pressure, which is very bad indeed to have during pregnancy. The placenta is apt to separate prematurely, causing severe bleeding. The placenta may not be adequate to support normal growth, and the baby may be malnourished in utero. Sometimes the kidneys of the mother function poorly, and the child dies in utero. It is a serious complication, and the obstetricians were watching very carefully the response to medication. They had the mother moved to Portland to be delivered in a hospital with a neonatal intensive care unit, because it was certain that she would not be able to go for her full nine months' gestation without the child dying prematurely.

At intervals she was given an oxytocin challenge test. Pitocin is given to stimulate the uterus to contract, and the fetal heart is closely monitored. If the heart rate falls sharply during a contraction, there is fetal distress, and an immediate Caesarian section must be done if the baby is to be born alive.

Mary Elizabeth was about two months premature, and

weighed one kilogram when she was hastily delivered that night. The mother had reported that her movements were less well felt than they had been, and an oxytocin challenge test was done, so the C-section was an emergency. There was not even time to inject the mother with cortisone to try to induce the enzyme which causes the lung to produce surfactant. Unless this is done and surfactant can be produced, a two pound infant born prematurely by C-section is almost certain to have hyaline membrane disease.

Mary Elizabeth in fact had this disease, which used to be almost always fatal. The lungs do not exchange oxygen well because of the hyaline membrane, and they have to be expanded by a ventilator. Now that ventilators have been improved, and attention is paid to important matters such as the oxygen saturation and pH of the blood, survival has risen to 80% in neonatal intensive care units.

Mary Elizabeth seemed to be doing quite well for a few days, then her platelets fell to dangerously low levels. As platelets in the blood are necessary for clotting to occur, she began to bleed. What apparently had happened was that either hypoxia or acidosis had set in motion a process of internal clotting of the blood, and the platelets had been used up. There are two mechanisms which are kept in balance by the body: one is the bleeding mechanism and the other the clotting mechanism. If either go wrong, the patient will bleed to death. Mary Elizabeth had a condition which is known as disseminated intravascular coagulation, because the components of the blood which are necessary for clotting are used up. Until they are replaced, the blood will remain fluid.

She was given a tranfusion of fresh frozen plasma and packed red blood cells. The danger in being born too soon always lies in the lungs. Unless they can be expanded and properly aerated, survival is not possible. The lungs became stiff and resistant to expansion because of the bleeding problem. The pressure from the respirator was increased, and she was given a dopamine drip to keep up her blood pressure. Finally, even at maximum pressure, the ventilator was not able to oxygenate her body, and on September 10th, when she was eleven days old, she finally died.

Astrologically, can we see why this child did not survive? The generally accepted rule is that the Sun, Moon and Ascendant must all be afflicted.

It must be pointed out that we do not yet know the astrological signature for death in infancy. The recent harmonic analysis of crib deaths in California has shown that Venus is unexpectedly important. Perhaps this is because Venus rules the function of adaptation.

The Acendant is in Gemini, a sign where, according to Dr. William Davidson, leakage of vitality occurs. The Ascendant ruler Mercury is at the midpoint Saturn-Pluto, and therefore very badly aspected. At death, the transiting Sun had reached Mercury.

The Moon is decreasing in light, and this is not good for vigor in infancy. The worst position for the Moon is for it to be in the last quarter, and here it is in the third quarter in a sign of fire. However, the ultimate cause of death was bleeding, and the Moon in Aries is said to signify the likelihood of this. Other indications in the chart must also be present, of course. At death, transiting Mars was square the natal Moon. Saturn was sesquiquadrate, that is the 135 degree aspect; the Moon and the Sun is quincunx, another important aspect in medical astrology.

The Sun is not severely afflicted. It has no close parallel, and the only mundane square is to Jupiter.

The prenatal eclipses give the answer. There was a solar eclipse in 14 Libra 23 on April 4, 1977. It fell square to the third cusp. The third house rules the lungs. If a child is to survive, its lungs, above all else, must funtion properly. If they had done so, the bleeding problem would not have arisen.

One might say that her physicians had Hobson's choice. It might have been better had they taken her mother to the operating room a little earlier. Taurus would have been rising, and the ruler Venus unafflicted. Perhaps some day we will be wise enough to choose the best birth time possible.

MARY ELIZABETH

43N 39
70W 16
Topocentric.

Born Aug. 30, 1977;
10.36 p.m. E.D.S.T.
Died Sept. 10, 1977; 10.01 p.m.
(Hospital record).

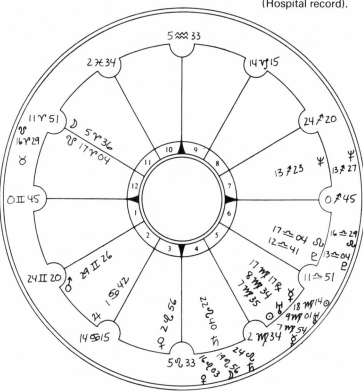

Declinations

Natal	Death
Sun 8 N 44	Sun 4 N 41
Moon 2 N 52	Moon 10 N 47
Mercury 0 N 54	Mercury 6 N 36
Venus 19 N 18	Venus 16 N 24
Mars 23 N 27	Mars 23 N 31
Jupiter 23 N 02	Jupiter 23 N 01
Saturn 14 N 57	Saturn 14 N 31
Uranus 13 S 57	Uranus 14 S 06
Neptune 20 S 56	Neptune 20 S 57
Pluto 10 N 19	Pluto 10 N 07

An Unfortunate Pair of Twins

Molly and Patricia were twins, born only four minutes apart. It is customary to deliver the second twin as quickly as possible after the first, to prevent asphyxia, which can happen if a breath of amniotic fluid is taken.

The hospital delivery room record notes that Molly was born at 5:18 p.m. and Patricia at 5:22 p.m. on April 22, 1970. They were approximately two months premature. Patricia died at the age of two days of hyaline membrane disease, and Molly survived, but will never be able to walk properly. She has cerebral palsy due to lack of oxygen either at birth or, more likely, in the newborn nursery. She has spastic diplegia. Her right leg has been operated on, and she has physical therapy twice a week and gets around on crutches.

As the charts of the twins are almost exactly the same, how do we explain why one died and one lived?

The difference lies solely with the house cusps, and we must look to them, and we must also use extremely small orbs, since there is less than a degree's difference on the Ascendant.

It is well known that the Moon is extremely important in infancy, and it must always be considered carefully. It can be seen that in Patricia's chart, the Moon is almost exactly conjunct the second cusp, and therefore afflicting the eighth, the House of Death.

Mercury is also almost within one degree of quincunx to the Ascendant, and the Ascendant is very close to the Moon-Pluto midpoint. These may all be factors to take into consideration, but I think we have to look further.

The Rule of Eclipes

Most of the old rules which have been passed down to us are useless, but I have found that eclipses really do work. The rule states that before birth, eclipses have a great influence on the developing foetus: "If one of the degrees of the zodiac held by the malefics at the eclipse before birth is rising at the time of birth, the child will not survive."

It is also, said (but I have been unable to confirm this) that lunar eclipses affect females more powerfully, and solar eclipses have more influence on males.

There were two eclipses shortly before the twins' birth. A solar eclipse on March 7, 1970 occured at 5:50 p.m. G.M.T. Mars at this time was in 0° Taurus 39. This therefore gives a sensitive point, which reacts for some time to transits.

At the time of death, Jupiter was at 0° Scorpio 39.

The lunar eclipse occured on February 21, 1970 at 8:44 a.m. G.M.T. Mars was then in 20 Aries 07. Patricia, who died, had her seventh cusp in 19 Aries 53. Remember that the delivery room record is only accurate to within a minute.

We see, therefore, that the old rule has not let us down. Eclipse Mars was opposite the Ascendant of the twin who died, and this point, the seventh cusp, takes away life and consciousness.

The position of Pluto at the March 7 eclipse is also significant. Pluto was in 26 Virgo 20, and this degree, under the Pole of the twelfth cusp, is conjunct within three minutes of arc (twelve seconds of time) to the natal twelfth cusp of Patricia.

Saturn was closely opposition Jupiter at the March 7 eclipse.

Both infants sustained brain damage (Jupiter rules the cerebral hemispheres of the brain) but only Patricia died, and the aspects in Molly's chart were not close enough to kill her.

PATRICIA

43N 39
70W 16

R.A.M.C. 115 49

5.22 p.m. E.S.T.
April 22, 1970.
Died on April 25, 1970.
(from hospital record).

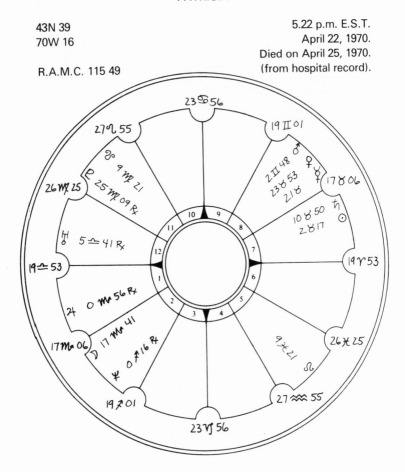

Topocentric.

MOLLY

43N 39
70W 16

5.18 p.m. E.S.T.
April 22, 1970.
(from hospital record).

R.A.M.C. 114 48

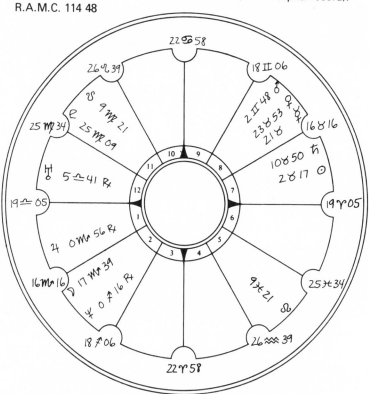

Topocentric.

A Child with One Brain

One would expect an unusual chart in the case of a child with one brain, for we have recently discovered that humans have two brains, normally interconnected, but with different functions and different personalities.

The left half of the brain is specialized for language. The right half of the brain does not understand language and cannot read, so in cases where the connection between the two halves has been cut, as in operations which have sometimes been performed to control certain types of epilepsy, only words in the right half of the visual field can be read. Why do we need the right brain? It seems that it is needed for all spatial abilities, drawing patterns, building blocks, recognizing faces, and grasping the total picture. In a split-brain person, where the connections have been severed, the left half often tries to do things which the right hand deplores. In the first such patient studied by psychologists, the left hand threatened the wife while the right hand tried to come to her rescue.

The right brain is thought to be the seat of mystical experience, since it is ineffable and cannot be expressed in words.

David was a normal child at birth, but at fourteen weeks was involved in a car accident in which the left cerebral hemisphere was destroyed. There are not many cases when this happens and the patient survives. It seems, however, that he will learn to compensate. It now has been found that the right brain can be taught to read, though not easily. The child is having special speech training, for the left hemisphere normally serves speech; but in cases where the left is destroyed early in life, the right hemisphere can be taught to do so. He is doing reasonably well.

There are several striking things about David's chart. In such an unusual case, one would expect to find a strong influence from a fixed star, and here Aldeberan rises. Aldeberan and Antares, which is placed in the opposite degree, Sagittarius 8° 39', are two of the four Royal Stars or Watchers of the Heavens among the Persians. They are both of the nature of Mars, and considered highly malefic. Their importance in this particular chart is brought out by the fact that the Sun on December 1st, the day of the accident, acted as the timing planet as it transited the degree held by Aldeberan.

Natal Uranus is in the eighteenth degree of Libra, a degree associated (together with the other degrees which are opposite it or square to it) with violence and danger.

Sagittarius rises. As I have stated in my Introduction to these cases, Jupiter rules the cerebral hemispheres of the brain which control the reasoning faculties of a human being. It is more likely, however, that Neptune, the co-ruler of Sagittarius, rules the right hemisphere, the hidden partner. It is therefore fortunate that Neptune is in aspect to the Sun. There is a Sun-Neptune paran square at lat. 44N. Although the process will be difficult, it is possible to develop the function of the right hemisphere because of this contact. Any contact with a significator, whether the aspect is hard or soft. The hard aspects—the traditional malefic aspects based on forty-five degrees—merely indicate greater difficulty.

The first house corresponds to the head. It is appropriate that, while terribly afflicted by Saturn in Gemini and Mars in Virgo, Sagittarius rises, containing its ruler, Jupiter the Preserver. We can therefore be certain that at the appropriate time, there would be severe injury to the head, and that it would cause damage to the left hemisphere of the brain. Mars and Saturn are the two planets most closely associated with Matter, and they have abolished the hemisphere most concerned with the skills we need to live in the world.

There are seven planets in mutable signs, which will help him to adapt very easily. Fire predominates, and he will not lack confidence and optimism. Everything except Jupiter is above Earth, so he will draw on others for his psychic energy.

He will be forced to develop the intuitive and creative side of his personality. Modern science has concentrated on developing the left hemisphere from the earlist days when the child first goes to school. Those who are creative and who cannot learn by the usual methods may find it difficult to learn to read. A brain hemisphere mis-match has been implicated in dyslexia. In a significant study by CT scan of the brain, normal controls are found to have a wider left parieto-occipital area, indicating a dominant left hemisphere. Dsylexics often have a dominant right hemisphere, with wider parieto-occipital areas on the right. As far as I know, this is the only way one can tell which hemisphere is dominant in a normal person.

There is no astrological rule for determining dominance, but most astrologers would look closely at Neptune and its aspects, particularly to the Moon. It would be very useful if the dominant right hemisphere types could be found and specially taught. Einstein himself was said not to be able to read until he was about eight years old.

I recently discussed this problem with Tony Joseph, who is a psychologist as well as an astrologer. He thinks that a clue may be found by the retrograde planets. "If the ruler of the Ascendant is retrograde at birth," he said, "the person will be an intuitive."

A recent statement in Carl Jansky's *Astrology, Nutritian and Health*, sent me to look at my charts to test a theory on the diagnosis of left-handedness in a horoscope. Left-handed people are very much more likely to be dominated by the right hemisphere. One sets up the chart with the position of the South Node of the Moon at the Ascendant. If there are more planets above than below the horizon, the statement was made that the native will be left-handed. This is not true, as anyone who tries it will quickly find out. However, it does seem that the ones who have more planets above the horizon in these charts are more creative. They may well be right hemisphere people.

DAVID

44N 06
70W 15

Sept. 16, 1972
at 1.01 p.m. E.D.S.T.
(data from father).

R.A.M.C. 180 15

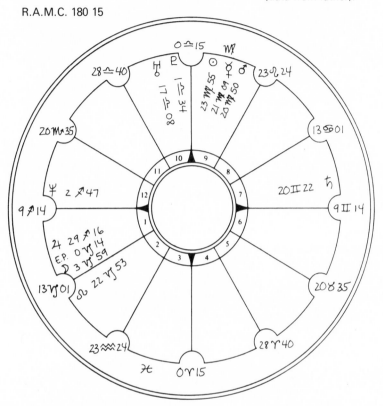

Declinations
No planets retrograde.
Sun 2 N 25
Moon 25 S 06
Mercury 5 N 04
Venus 16 N 47
Mars 4 N 33
Jupiter 23 S 27
Saturn 21 N 30
Uranus 6 S 16
Neptune 19 S 08
Pluto 13 N 52

Topocentric.

Car accident Dec. 1, 1972 at 44N 06, 70W 15.

It is becoming apparent that the values of the West and the values of the East must be melded if mankind is to progress. Some are striving to follow this path, but most of them have not as yet had much influence on society because they are not old enough. Meditation is a way to develop the right hemisphere, and we can expect to see an expansion of consciousness in most people in another generation. We have to use both hemispheres. It is interesting that the existence of the 'silent partner,' the right side of the brain, was not even suspected until recently. Was this because we were not at the stage where we could profitably utilize this knowledge? Astrologers claim that the influence of the outer planets was only felt fully after they had been discovered. Perhaps some law of this kind is operating here. The cosmic destiny of this child may be to lead the way to an understanding of the secret life of the soul.

Jupiter Combust

I was on duty one night when Paul came into the emergency room with a temperature of 106°. It is said that the protein of the brain is coagulated at 108°, so I lost no time in admitting and cooling him. The cultures taken from his blood, urine, throat, and spinal fluid were all negative, so we never made a diagnosis except that he must have had a virus infection.

At 8 a.m. the next morning he stopped breathing, and we had to resuscitate him. No heart beat could be heard during this episode. His blood pressure must have fallen to zero, because his kidneys shut down due to the lack of oxygen, and he produced no urine for a month. It was touch and go for a while, as he was in deep coma, supported by dialysis and intravenous fluids throughout this time. If a patient can be kept alive until the kidneys regenerate, they will appear to be normal thereafter. He gradually regained consciousness and seemed to be recovering. Paul's mother sat with him all day in the intensive care unit, and after a month he had recovered enough to know her and to cry when she left him. He was only three years old.

We had not known him before his illness, but it seemed to us when we sent him home that he had sustained some brain damage due to the fever or due to the episode of respiratory arrest.

Three months later, Paul began to show signs of a degenerative muscle disease. His gait staggered and finally he could not walk at all. Next his arms became weak and finally his speech muscles failed. A febrile illness followed by a latent period and then increasing paralysis does not fit any known disease pattern. We could not even be certain there was any link at all between these events. He was readmitted to the hospital on December 12, 1968.

We fed him by stomach tube, since he could not swallow. Finally another very strange and unforeseen event occurred. His brain lost control of the mechanism for regulating temperature and his temperature rose to 108° before he died at 1:40 a.m. on December 22. Malignant hyperthermis, which is what it appeared to be, is now known to be linked in some way with abnormal muscle enzymes. Here one would expect to see the influence of Mars.

His mother had previously lost a baby who died at the age of three months with pneumonia. It is possible that there was a hereditary immune deficiency in both children. Recently I saw in the local paper that she had been granted a divorce and I am sure that her life was irrevocably altered by the double tragedy.

The natal chart of Paul is severely afflicted. An old axiom states that if the Sun and Moon are both connected with baleful fixed stars, the child will not grow up. Here the Moon is with Algol and the Sun with Aldeberan.

Neptune rises. This is said to weaken the body. Mars conjunct Pluto conjunct Uranus opposition Saturn and square Venus must be considered very evil.

If one looks at the natal chart, the most afflicted houses are the eleventh and fifth, which hold Mars and Saturn and are square Venus in the eighth house. This tells us at once that there will be circulatory failure causing electrolyte problems, and that there will be a breakdown of the excretory function since the eighth house is involved. This is what happened.

Mercury, the ruler of the eighth house, is natally conjunct the Moon, and transiting Neptune was in oppostion when he first became ill. Transiting Pluto was square natal Venus, already afflicted, and transiting Mars and natal Venus were in parallel.

PAUL

43N 39
70W 16

Born May 29, 1965
at 5.10 p.m. E.D.S.T.
(hospital record).

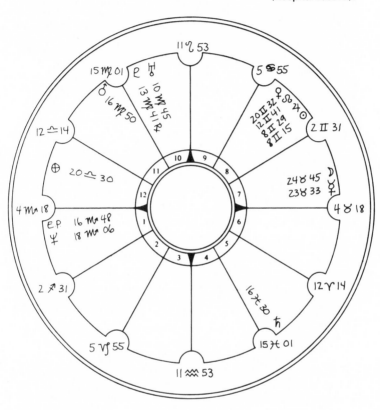

Declinations.
Sun 21 N 41
Moon 17 N 39
Mercury 17 N 23
Venus 23 N 48
Mars 6 N 13
Saturn 6 N 59
Jupiter 21 N 11
Uranus 8 N 15
Neptune 15 S 29
Pluto 19 N 37

Topocentric.

PAUL

Episode of shock with subsequent renal failure.

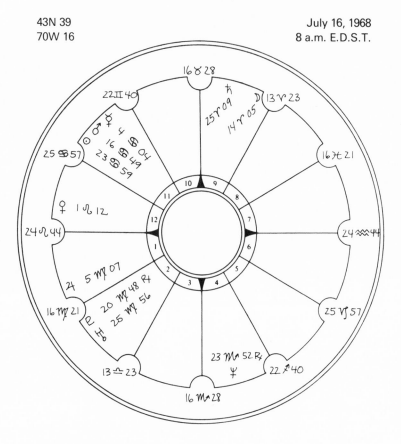

43N 39
70W 16

July 16, 1968
8 a.m. E.D.S.T.

Declinations.   Topocentric
Sun 21 N 19
Moon 5 N 38
Mercury 21 N 41
Venus 21 N 32
Mars 23 N 18
Jupiter 10 35
Saturn 7 N 25
Uranus 2 N 17
Neptune 17 03
Pluto 17 N 25

PAUL

43N 39
70W 16

Death Chart. 1.40 a.m.
Dec. 22, 1968 E.S.T.

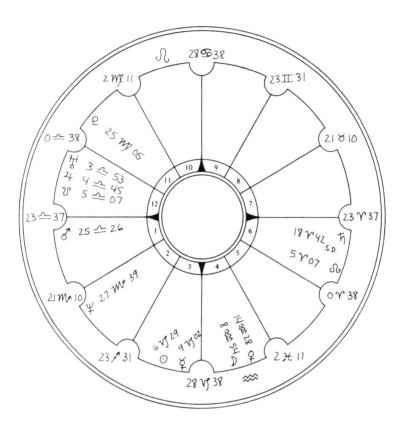

Declinations

Sun 23 S 27
Moon 22 S 55
Mercury 25 S 13
Venus 18 S 25
Mars 8 S 35

Saturn 4 N 56
Uranus 0 S 51
Neptune 17 S 58
Pluto 16 N 06

Topocentric.

Lunation 27 Sag. 29
Dec. 18, 1968
Decl. 23 S 25

The most significant aspect at death is a 'mundane opposition' of Neptune to Sun and Jupiter, and ascensional direction which I explain in the last and most difficult part of this book. There is no zodiacal opposition, but Neptune is in the second house and its 'oblique ascension' is exactly opposite that of this natal conjunction, which in 'oblique ascension' is exact.

A planet close to the Sun is said to be combust and shorn of its power to assist the native. Jupiter is combust and Jupiter rules the brain; while Mars was rising at death, a fiery conflagration in this child's body burned him up, extinguishing his life.

A Case Of Leukemia

This is the story of Robin, who died of leukemia. I have related the history of her sister Laurie in Chapter 28: *The Many Faces of Love.* The death of Robin had an emotional impact far beyond her immediate environment and was responsible for the way her family treated Laurie, the substitute child, for whom nothing was too good. Laurie is a nymphomaniac and neurotic, who in turn influences her baby, and so the neuroses are passed down through the generations.

Her mother married late in life and was thirty-seven when the second child Robin was born, delivered by Caesarian section like her older brother. Her mother, on seeing her for the first time, said that she knew she would not live to grow up, but it may have been after Robin died that she said this, for no one could have guessed to see her that she was destined to die young. She was the picture of health and vitality.

Children who are seriously ill often are very brave and uncomplaining. Although she was in hospital a great part of her last year of life, and had many drugs which made her weak and nauseated, and many blood transfusions, she complained less about dying than her sister Laurie complains about her headaches and stomach aches.

Leukemia was diagnosed quite by chance. Both she and her brother became ill with mumps encephalitis, and were admitted to hospital. Routine blood count showed that Robin was in the early stages of lymphatic leukemia and she was sent to Boston for treatment. At that time, she was two years nine months, and she appeared to be healthy and vigorous.

The X-rays her mother had when she was pregnant may have contributed to her illness, for leukemia is more common among children prenatally exposed to radiation, which was almost routine in suspected cases of pelvic disproportion. Malignant disease remains a challenge to the astrologer. Probably each of the many types has its own astrological signature. If any planet is more important than another, it is Neptune; because Neptune rules the general immunity of the body and the recognition of the self and non-self. Malignant cells, though derived from the body tissues, grow in a wild and unregulated manner, and if immune surveillance is adequate, they should be recognized as aberrant and destroyed. Uranus plays a part, since Saturn and Uranus are ancient enemies, and Saturn maintains form and structure; whereas Uranus rules that which is discontinuous with the past and has arisen unexpectedly, for example mutations. X-rays, which cause mutations, are under Uranus.

In Robin's case, there are many striking features in the chart of birth and the progressions and transits at death. Leo rises. According to Charles Carter, Leo is a strong sign in adult life but weak in childhood, and is the most common Ascendant in cases of infant mortality. The Sun, which is the Ascendant ruler, is in paran square to the Moon and Neptune. The Sun-Pluto midpoint equals this Neptune-Moon conjunction.

According to Ebertin, Sun-Pluto signifies the regeneration of the cell. The Moon-Neptune conjunction is in paran square to Uranus. Neptune, with so many prominent aspects, is the most important significator in lymphatic leukemia, the *T*-cell lymophocytes being under the thymus, which is ruled by Neptune. She had a *T*-cell leukemia, the most fatal kind. The cell is ruled by the Sun, and the blood, a fluid, by the Moon. Her impending death was heralded by the eclipse of February 5, 1962 in 15 Aquarius 44 on her seventh cusp. Mars is in a close square to Mercury, and a feature of her illness was the extremely high temperatures up to 107°. In the end this caused her death. The nodes are square the East Point and Venus is sextile, with Jupiter sextile Saturn. The worst aspect is the parallel of Mars, Jupiter and Uranus.

Mars and Jupiter, being fiery planets, burnt her up, as happened in the case of the little boy Paul in *Jupiter Combust*.

ROBIN

43N 39
70W 16

R.A.M.C. 32 22

Born 8.34 a.m. E.D.S.T.
June 26, 1958;
(hospital record).
Died June 11, 1962 time unknown.

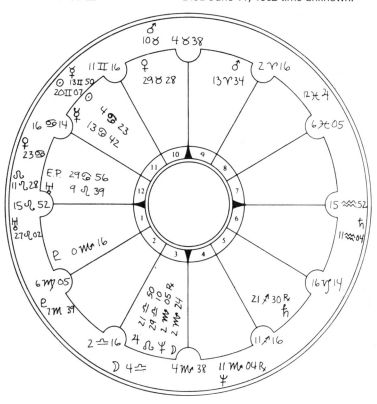

Transits on day of death, outer ring.

Topocentric

Declinations
Sun 23 N 23
Moon 12 S 02
Mercury 24 N 36
Venus 18 N 07
Mars 3 N 07
Jupiter 7 S 18
Saturn 21 S 46
Uranus 18 N 34
Neptune 10 S 32
Pluto 11 N 28

The secondary progressions at death show that the Moon has progressed from the conjunction with Neptune to the conjunction with Saturn, and the transiting Sun opposes this point. There is also a Grand Square at death between transiting Mars, natal Uranus, transiting nodes, transiting Neptune, and transiting Saturn. These all afflict Uranus, the ruler of the seventh house, and thus affect the 1-7 axis giving a brain death.

I believe that the thirteenth harmonic is connected with death. The thirteenth harmonic position of the Sun is 27 Leo with transiting Uranus and the thirteenth harmonic position of Neptune is 27 Scorpio. I have found Uranus prominent in the thirteenth harmonic charts of others who have died of cancer, but no investigations of the thirteenth harmonic have been published.

Why Johnnie Could Not Draw

The last time I saw Johnnie was when he had his pre-school physical. When I examine the five year olds who are just about to enter kindergarten, I ask them to draw a man. The extremely immature ones will hang their heads and refuse. Some will draw pictures which are so bizarre that you wonder what can be going on in the mind of the child. Johnnie drew a man which was so small that I could hardly see it. He was the normal twin and his brother Joe was the sickly one who had all the attention of the family from the age of three months. Johnnie feels small and insignificant.

This case is very baffling. There is only five minutes difference in the birth times, and yet there is all the difference in the world between the modes of expression of the planetary energies in the two cases. The only difference in the charts is that the house cusps are approximately a degree apart and the most important point is the Ascendant with its aspects, since it is representative of the body.

Until the age of three months, both twins grew and developed normally. Then Joe began to have seizures, and was admitted to the hospital in *status epilepticus*, a potentially fatal disorder in which the seizures are so continuous that the brain cannot get enough oxygen; and unless the seizures can be stopped, the patient will die.

Astrologically speaking, one would expect one twin to have the Ascendant-Descendant axis afflicted at this time of attack on the body. Also Mercury and Neptune, rulers in general of the nervous system and states of unconsciousness, which are closely involved with this axis, while the other twin would have the natural rulers of the function of nurture afflicted. (10-4 axis and Saturn and the Moon). The home conditions must have been chaotic. None of the consultants called in knew what was going on and the only suggestion they could make was to send the child to specialists in Boston.

I was the pediatric resident on duty the night Joey was admitted. We first tried to stop his seizures with phenobarb and Dilantin, then we sought the cause. It turned out to be hypoglycemia, the rarest cause in children of this age.

It is known that newborn infants can have a very low blood sugar without seizures, although no one knows why this is so. Joey was three months old, and therefore no longer fell into the newborn category. His blood sugar was so low that we thought the lab must have made an error and repeated it. It was 15 mg. at first, and only 5 mg. the second time. This is supposed to be incompatible with life. He did not die, but unfortunately suffered severe brain damage, which is irreversible.

The problem which was never solved satisfactorily, was the mechanism of the hypoglycemia. We pondered all the possible causes. Was it a case of glycogen storage disease, a rare and fatal genetic defect in which the stored glycogen cannot be converted to glucose? Was it an insulinoma, a tumor of the pancreas which pours out insulin unceasingly and which does not turn itself off when the supply is sufficient? Was it due to sepsis, which stresses the body and uses up glucose? Was it due to lack of growth hormone? Was it ketotic hypoglycemia, which is only found in young children, usually between two to six years? Was it leucine sensitivity?

Joey was sent to Boston for the answers. His mother commenced a dreadful period of driving to Boston to see him and trying to look after Johnnie and her four year old daughter at home. It was impossible to make a diagnosis. The presumptive evidence was for a number of scattered wild cells in the pancreas, producing insulin in excess, in fact, an insulinoma, but not in a circumscribed area where it could be removed surgically.

He was sent home on an experimental drug, diazoxide, which kept his blood sugar reasonably normal, but his mother also had to feed him with a high protein—low carbohydrate diet every three or four hours day and night. His seizure threshold was low . . . he seized easily, and was not completely controlled, even with maximum doses of Dilantin.

Hypoglycemia is still a confusing disease, especially in children. There are many metabolic pathways by which the needs of the brain and body can be met. There are two organs which use glucose, but do not need insulin in order to get it into their cells. These are the brain and the red blood cells.

During fasting, the insulin level falls. This is the normal fail safe mechanism to ensure survival. The available glucose goes to the blood and brain, where it is most needed. In an adult, the brain needs one hundred grams of glucose daily for its energy, and this is about a quarter of the total energy needs of the body in a resting state. Babies need more proportionately, as they have more brain substance in relation to the body.

There are stores of glycogen in the liver and muscles, totalling two hundred fifty grams, which can be converted to glucose when the body is not taking it in. We also manufacture glucose by several pathways with the help of enzymes. The end products of the contraction of muscle, pyruvic and lactic acids, can be turned back into glycogen. The red blood cells also produce lactate when they use up glucose. If there is an enzyme defect in the liver, it cannot convert the lactate and pyruvate in this way and hypoglycemia may result.

Normally, the liver of course manufactures glycogen from the food coming into the body. Yet during a fast, the supply of glucose to the brain must be kept up, and glucose is then made from protein and fat taken out of the body. We need the adrenocortical hormone to do this, and if it is insufficient, as in Addison's disease, hypoglycemia will result. The sympathetic nervous system, mediated through epinephrine, stimulates adrenocortical hormone production. Anyone who has fasted for several days will be aware of the rapid heart rate and other signs of sympathetic nervous system over-activity unless sweetened drinks are taken.

It can be seen how complex hypoglycemia is — even the experts in Boston were puzzled. Finally they decided that his pancreas should be removed. This would have meant lifelong diabetes and his parents would not give their consent, especially since it was obvious that his brain was already badly damaged. They compromised and removed half. The half pancreas was packed in dry ice and flown to Denmark, where one of the world's foremost authorities on infantile hypoglycemia has his research lab. No insulinoma was found.

A careful examination of Joseph's chart shows some close aspects to the Ascendant which his twin does not have. The Sun is semisquare the Ascendant, and the nodes of the Moon are parallel it. The Ascendant falls at the midpoint of Jupiter and Uranus, given by Ebertin as seizures.

The eclipse of September 22 fell at 29 Virgo 31. The midpoint of Mars and Jupiter, which is said to be connected with hypoglycemia, is in 14 Leo 12 in both charts. It is more significant in Joseph's chart, since it is in close aspect to an angle, the fourth cusp. The eclipse point fell 45° away from this midpoint, and the semisquare is powerful in medical astrology.

The important configuration in the charts is the Y formation between Saturn in the eighth house (metabolism), Neptune in the third, and Uranus in the first. Both the first and third houses are connected with the brain and consciousness. Of course, this does not explain why one twin should have incurred brain damage due to a disordered metabolic process and not the other. One can only suppose that the three powerful aspects to the Ascendant in the case of the affected twin were responsible.

The timing was interesting. Transiting Neptune had closed to form the exact 150° aspect to Saturn in the eighth house. Transiting Jupiter had come to the conjunction of natal Uranus. Transiting Pluto was in semisquare to the natal Saturn-Neptune midpoint at 9 Leo 36, said to be the point of chronic illness. Mercury was in 15 Libra 54, at the Neptune-Jupiter midpoint. In the secondary progressions, the Ascendant was in 26 Scorpio and therefore accentuated the natal Y formation.

As Joey grew older, his hypoglycemia improved. He wears braces, and attends the special school for children with cerebral palsy. Of course, his brain is very damaged, and he

JOSEPH

43N 39; 70W 16.

First twin, born 9.23 a.m.
E.D.S.T. July 24, 1968;
(hospital record).

R.A.M.C. 72 49

Johnnie born 9.28 a.m.

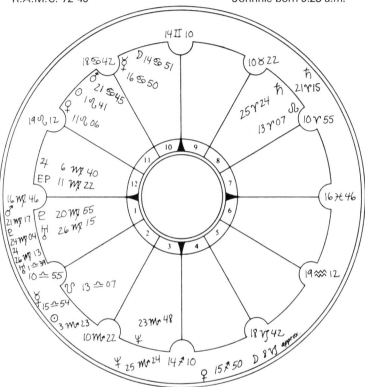

Transits on Oct. 26, 1968, in outer ring-onset of seizures.

Topocentric

Declinations
Sun 19 N 57
Moon 27 N 36
Mercury 22 N 29
Venus 18 N 53
Mars 22 N 37
Jupiter 10 N 03
Saturn 7 N 28
Uranus 2 N 09
Neptune 17 S 02
Pluto 17 N 20

will never be able to do much with his life. Johnnie goes to the local school and is now in the fourth grade. I saw his mother with her new daughter at my Well-Baby Clinic last month. I have not seen Johnnie for several years, but last time I saw him, he could not draw. One wonders how much psychological damage was done to him at the time that his twin almost died.

The Luck Of The Irish

Elizabeth O'Hara's mother was nineteen years old and had previously had two abortions. Unfortunately, with this pregnancy she had no prenatal care, and Elizabeth came too soon.

Hospital policy is to resucitate any infant born alive and transfer it to the nursery in a warmed incubator. Elizabeth was so small that the intern wrapped her in a blanket, carried her down the corridor, and handed her to the nurse with the remark, "I doubt if this one is viable." She weighed one pound thirteen ounces (eight hundred forty grams) and the gestation period was estimated at just over twenty weeks.

In the old days, five years ago, if a baby was not fed for twenty-four hours, the blood sugar became very low, and since the brain depends on sugar for its metabolism, seizures and cerebral palsy could result.

Elizabeth was put into a warmed incubator, and an umbilical catheter was inserted. She could now be nourished with 10% glucose in water, and intravenous medication was given.

The other main cause of cerebral palsy is brain damage due to insufficient oxygen. These infants do not have a well developed respiratory drive, and are apt to stop breathing for several minutes at a time. An apnea monitor is attached to the chest to trigger an alarm when this happens. A nurse then stimulates the child by rocking the water bed or stroking the skin. These three simple measures, prompt rewarming, early nourishment, and prevention of apnea, have doubled the survival rate of small babies and decreased the incidence of brain damage in the survivors.

However, there is a price to be paid for the early feeding. There is great danger of fluid overload, since all nourishment at first must be given intravenously. An enormous increase in the incidence of *patent ductus* has been reported throughout the United States in the last few years. This has been produced by overhydration, and it is the price we pay.

Normally at birth when the umbilical cord is tied and the infant breathes, the lungs expand and become full of air. Before birth, they are solid and airless of course. Before birth the blood does not pass through the lungs to receive oxygen. A bypass (the ductus) conducts blood which is on its way to the lungs through a short connection which leads back to the aorta, whence it is circulated to the rest of the body. After birth when the lungs become full of air, the pressure in them falls. The blood can now flow freely from the heart into the lungs and the ductus closes spontaneously in most cases.

If it remains open, the lungs will receive too much blood; for not only do they have to deal with the normal amount but in addition they receive some blood through the ductus which reverses its direction of flow from an area of high pressure— the body— to an area of low pressure— the lungs. The lungs then become flooded with blood and are damaged. The pressure in them rises and this increase of pressure can never be reversed. The child will die.

Hence if we get a ductus which does not close spontaneously, we must tie it off in the operating room. This should be done in the first ten days or two weeks of life. If it is left for five or six weeks, the lungs will be so damaged that the child will die at three months or thereabouts.

Elizabeth was nine days old and unbelievably small when they took her to surgery. Her chart at the beginning of the operation is shown beside the natal chart. As you can guess, the operation was successful. Three weeks later she was off oxygen, breathing on her own, and being fed through a tube placed in her stomach. She had regained her birth weight. At two months, she weighed three pounds thirteen ounces, and was taking formula from a bottle.

It is now possible to keep infants of seven hundred grams and over (but none under this weight) from dying in the first few days. The final answer about their brain development is not yet known. If they can be protected from damage due to lack of oxygen and a low blood sugar, they seem to be normal. The passage of Uranus into Scorpio marked the advent of a new kind and quality of care for the newborn. Neonatal intensive care units have been opened in all the big centers.

Astrologically, the chart is a bit of a puzzler. The Moon conjuncts Neptune, and this is traditionally considered a dangerous aspect which lowers vitality. It is opposition the eighth cusp and the midpoint of Mars-Venus. The Ascendant is in Scorpio, which is not supposed to be a very strong sign, and moreover it is square Saturn. Venus in the eighth house is sesquiquadrate Uranus in the twelfth. The ruler of the eighth house, Mercury, is semisquare the Mars-Saturn midpoint.

A Western astrologer faced with this chart and a one pound thirteen ounce premature child would not hold out much hope for it. Probably the Indian astrologers are more skilled than we are in determining whether death is likely. I am therefore putting the chart into the sidereal zodiac with equal houses from the Ascendant, and also calculating its ninth harmonic, the *Navamsa*, to see if we can make a better prediction using their methods. Hindu astrology has different rules for interpretation. These give a brighter picture and seem quite apt for the persistance of fetal circulation and the danger to the lungs which Elizabeth had. They use a system by which a planet is benefic or malefic according to chart position. The Ascendant lord is always benefic. The lords of the signs on the cusps of the ninth and fifth houses are also benefic, even though they may be natural malefics. Planets in the angles and the ninth and fifth houses help the native.

The Navamsa chart is more important than the natal, and if there is conflict, the indications shown in the *Navamsa* will prevail. In the *Navamsa* chart, with Mars rising in Aries, the Sun is lord of the fifth and Jupiter of the ninth. Mars rules the eighth house. His action here is to help the native through surgery, not to kill. The Nodes take the characterisitic of the lord of the sign wherein they are placed. Since the Dragon's Head in the *Navamsa* is in Leo, it is benefic, since the Sun is

Elizabeth O'Hara

Sidereal Zodiac with Navamsa outside

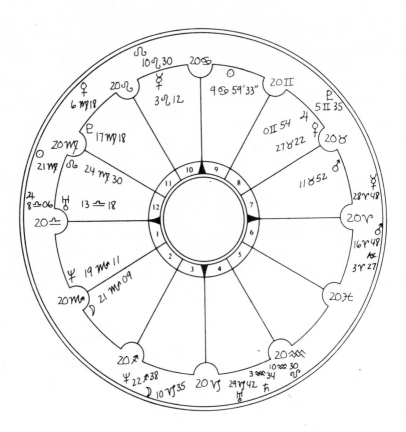

Natal   on 5th cusp of Navamsa (ruler Navamsa 3rd)
Navamsa   on 11th cusp of Navamsa

ELIZABETH

43N39
70W 16

Born 2.19 p.m.
July 26, 1977 E.D.S.T.
(hospital record).

R.A.M.C. 148 49

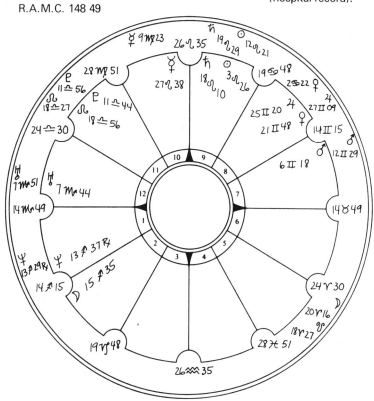

Topocentric.

Transits in outer ring-surgery at 9.20 p.m. Aug. 4, 1977.

benefic. *Navamsa* Jupiter and Moon are in square, which is highly beneficial, since it is the nature of the planets, not the aspect, which counts. The opposition of Jupiter to the beneficent Mars is also good. Note that the natal Sun is in Cancer in the ninth, and the Navamsa Moon is in opposition to it.

The Hindu astrologers also use the chart with the natal Moon rising, and judge death from its eighth house. Here the Sun occupies the eighth, helping to prolong life. If we put the *Navamsa* Moon on the Ascendant, the *Navamsa* Dragon's Head, a benefic here, is on the eighth cusp. The Moon is poorly placed in the signs of her fall and debility in both the *Navamsa* and the natal charts. The chief malefic is Saturn. He is placed precisely on the 11th cusp of the Navamsa chart, the house which denotes circulation of the blood. Natal Mercury, which in the *Navamsa* chart rules the lungs, is in exact opposition.

Although Elizabeth has survived against all odds, one cannot help wondering how she will fare when she is sent home to her young mother. Her Moon, after all, is very poorly placed.

I would surmise that since Venus, the lord of the Ascendant, is trine *Navamsa* Uranus in the fourth house, everything in her home circumstances will turn out for the best in a surprising and unforeseen manner.

So far, Elizabeth has had a charmed life, having been born so close to a neonatal intensive care unit with a Mayo Clinic trained pediatric cardiologist in attendance. She has also had great luck— the luck of the Irish.

Ancient Wisdom

The wisdom of the past held that man was a being of body, soul and spirit.

It was recognized that man was part of the organism of the planet Earth, that the well being of both were completely intertwined, and furthermore, that the Earth, planets and stars were part of an immense system which was in perfect harmony.

Man knew that he could attune himself to the creative Intelligence of the living Universe. There were centers of initiation where this was taught.

The entire surface of the Earth is marked with the traces of a gigantic work of prehistoric engineering, the remains of a once universal system of natural magic, involving the use of polar magnetism together with another force related to solar energy.

Modern research has revealed that the stone monuments of prehistoric antiquity are not the work of primitive barbarians, but the scientific instruments of an advanced universal civilization. Relics which survive are the "ley" system and the aligned monuments of Britain. The leys are old tracks, footpaths and traditional boundaries which cross Britain and run through all the old sacred places. It seemed that churches, crosses, holy wells, stone circles and other places of worship were placed on the lines of great geometrical figures which were themselves constructed in relation to the positions of the heavenly bodies. Lines set at an angle of 6 degrees north of due East joined centers dedicated to the

Moon cult of the West with those of the Sun cult in the East.

It has been suggested that some forgotten principle was involved, as the technology used to build and lay out these lines must have served some purpose to enrich human life. It is felt that stone circles acted as receiving centers for direct influence from heavenly constellations that were known by the priesthood, and that these were activated at certain seasons of the year.

It seems they knew much about what we know as astrology and which has since been forgotten.

At the time of an eclipse, the magnetic field of the Earth was altered, so that it became very important to be able to predict eclipses in advance. Stonehenge 1 was designed for this purpose. It is dated, according to Fred Hoyle, at 1800 B.C.

In China, where the same system of straight lines called dragon paths exists, it is considered that the place of burial is very important. Favorable sites are on high ground, preferably close to a stream, and facing south, with higher ground behind. It must be at the meeting point of the yin current, which ran over low ground, and the yang current, which ran over high round.

The place of birth was also considered important. From my charts I have noticed that almost every child who died had been born in the smallest hospital in the area. It stands on low ground, over what was once a swamp. Only about 5-10% of local births are in this hospital. The largest hospital stands on high ground, and is obviously on a yang line, with a beautiful view of distant mountains. The geomantic influence of the place of birth has never been mentioned in Western literature, as far as I am aware, but is probably important.

I am convinced that the Cosmos is a giant computer. We are computed in at birth, and out at death. In a later chapter, I will set forward some evidence that supports this point of view.

It is astrological evidence, but nothing like the astrology we use everyday.

The Cosmos, A Computer

In 1964 and 1965, an extraordinary series of articles was published in *Spica*, a British astrological journal. At the time, I was searching for a way to predict in advance when a child would be born. A sentence in one of the articles by Nelson Page leaped to my attention. "There is always an exact genealogical connection between the charts of parents and child," it said. "An O.A. point, transposed to the date and time of the birth of the child, of the parent will always be exactly conjunct, or exactly opposite, and O.A. point of the child."

This meant nothing to me, since I had no idea what the author meant by an O.A. point or how it was transposed. I set out to study the articles, and it took me five years to prove that the statement was true.

The most difficult part was in learning to calculate the O.A. (Oblique Ascension) and O.D. (Oblique Descension) points. The astrology we use is two dimensional. The ecliptic, or zodiac, we use gives planetary positions in degrees, minutes, and seconds of the signs. We know about latitude and declination, but few of us use them.

In order to calculate the position in three dimensions, longitude, latitude, and declination are all necessary. Latitude is the distance North or South of the narrow band of the ecliptic, the apparent pathway of the Sun through the signs of the zodiac. The Sun has no latitude, but the Moon, Venus, and Pluto may have great latitude, and the other planets have some, although it is not very much.

It stands to reason that if a planet has North latitude, its body will rise over the horizon before the degree of the zodiac it is in, which has zero latitude and is therefore further South. If the planet has South latitude, it will rise later than the degree of the zodiac it is in. The difference between these times is the ascensional difference, and depends on the latitude of the place on the Earth's surface and the declination of the planet.

Alan Leo gives the rules for calculating the right ascension and the semiarc, which are both needed if one is to find the oblique ascension of a planet. As most people would rather not calculate them, Neil Michelson will do the computation for about two dollars—a great bargain.

It must be realized that we are working with two circles, the circle of the Ecliptic around its center, with the degrees of the zodiac, and the circle of the Equator, which is the projection on the sky of the Earth's equator. Since the plane of the orbit of the Earth is inclined at an angle of 23° 27' to that of the ecliptic, they do not coincide. Right ascension is measured along the celestial Equator and declination above and below it.

Primary Directions, being based on the rotation of the Earth around its axis, are measured in Right Ascension. The two circles cross at 0 Aries, when the Sun has zero declination. It is probable that we could abolish the Ecliptic and work only with declination. The complaint of sidereal astrologers that we are using the wrong zodiac is therefore meaningless.

Sidereal Time can also be called the Right Ascension of the Midheaven (R.A.M.C.) and as 15° is equal to one hour, we divide the sidereal time by fifteen to find the number of degrees and minutes and seconds on the midheaven. Transposition to a different place and time is simple:

R.A.M.C. event minus R.A.M.C. birth equals arc of transpostion.

This is added to all the birth O.A. or O.D. positions. The R.A.M.C. obtained is that of the EVENT. The planetary positions are those of the BIRTH transposed to the EVENT.

These are then compared with the planetary positions of the event and if the event is the birth of a child, one of the planetary positions will coincide.

In practice, the original method has been simplified. If a planet is exactly on the midheaven at birth- or at any distance from it, say x degrees, it will be in exactly the same position, x degrees away, after it has been transposed.

One has only to compare the positions with regard to their distances from the midheaven to see if an 'exact contact' is made.

This method is much easier to calculate than the original, and its formula is as follows:

Meridian Distance (measured in degrees of R.A. from the M.C. or I.C. whichever is appropriate) divided by Semiarc (nocturnal or diurnal) multiplied by ninety equals the M.Do, which is the true distance in oblique ascension from the midheaven or I.C.

The O.A./O.D. points used are those of the planets, the house cusps, the Part of Fortune (which combines the influence of the Sun, Moon, and Ascendant, and is particularly important in genealogical contacts) and the Mean Lunar Node.

One of the points which has a most powerful genealogical value is the Mean Node of the Moon—not the true Node!

The Moon with the Earth form a pair which together orbit around the Sun. They spin around a center of gravity which is common to both. As seen from the Sun, it is the center of gravity which is valid, and this has a triple significance, obtaining power from the Earth, Sun and Moon.

More or less the same reasoning applies to the Part of Fortune. I had never used it, but after studying Topocentric methods, I am convinced that it is valid in genealogical contacts.

In order to show how orbless astrology works out in practice, I am presenting the charts of two parents and their children, Martha, Mary, and Michael. The birth times of all of them were fairly accurately known. The mother has been discussed in Chapter 16.

Father M.Do's			House cusps		Mother M.Do's		
R.A.M.C.	105	42	For all charts		R.A.M.C.	36	
Sun	85	25	11th	30	Sun	36	40
Moon	33	36	12th	60	Moon	1	30
Mercury	66	33	2nd	60	Mercury	53	02
Venus	46	13	3rd	30	Venus	32	01
Mars	23	29			Mars	14	21
Jupiter	87	30			Jupiter	86	40
Saturn	4	03			Saturn	64	25
Uranus	30	34			Uranus	64	38
Neptune	13	34			Neptune	81	24
Pluto	12	07			Pluto	51	07
Fortuna	37	18			Fortuna	48	09
Node	9	50			Node	4	29

It was necessary to have one chart which was exact in order to rectify the others. The chart of the father was chosen. It was rectified by primary directions by the Topocentric method. Primary directions are calculated by directing the Promittor under the pole of the Significator, according to Kuhn's method, and using the arc of 59' 08" per year, based on the rotation of the Earth.

In the chart of a man, aspects of the Sun or Mars to angles or the 5-11 cusps, or the 2-8th cusps (very important in matters connected with sex and family relationships) are found to correspond to the births of children. Mars square Ascendant was the primary direction for the birth of the first daughter, Martha. It equated within two days to an R.A.M.C. of 105 ° 42'.

The fifth cusp directed to the trine of Venus corresponded with marriage, with the same R.A.M.C. Uranus to the fourth cusp corresponded with the second marriage.

If one is not using an accurate chart, one soon knows it, as the other charts with which it is being compared do not come out accurately. It is like solving a crossward puzzle.

There are perfect contacts between all five charts.

The contact between Martha's Node and her father's Saturn gave her his New England work ethic. She is the only one of the three who has settled down to earn a living.

In contrast to her sister and her brother, Martha has not asked for journeys around the world. She is working as a civil servant, and paying off her graduate school debt.

The 12/2 house cusp contact of her mother with her Neptune operates to make her supersensitive. She cries easily, and is apt to brood. As one would expect from Scorpio rising, she is the most reserved of the three. She does not have the good looks of her sister, or the flamboyance of her brother. She is quiet, sober, and reliable, with strong family ties.

The Venus-Jupiter contact between Mary and her father give her his good looks and willowy figure. One would never guess that she has never had any interest in anyone of the opposite sex. This is probably due to the influence of her mother, who is so self-conscious that she cannot make any human contacts at all, let alone with men. Mary does not seem anxious to enter the everyday world of work. A summer as a waitress gave her enough to go travelling. Her mother, who thinks nothing too good for her, encourages her to think vaguely about medical school, for which she has not the slightest background. The second house Fortuna contact is operating.

Martha			*Mary*			*Michael*		
R.A.M.C	144	45	R.A.M.C.	290	24	R.A.M.C.	272	49
Sun	70	04		42	09		59	23
Moon	57	17		20	30		40	52
Mercury	84	50		52	16		33	10
Venus	70	48		14	47		87	32
Mars	36	33		63	40		21	02
Jupiter	84	45		46	13		66	21
Saturn	56	55		83	08		40	26
Uranus	27	56		1	19		37	18
Neptune	60			86	47		71	11
Pluto	2	54		52	40		80	58
Fortuna	47	08		60			81	24
Node	4	03		42	54		26	50

LUKE

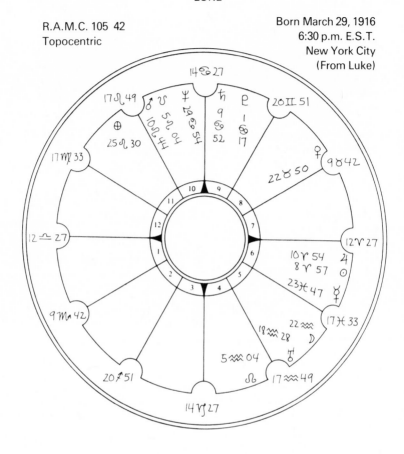

R.A.M.C. 105 42
Topocentric

Born March 29, 1916
6:30 p.m. E.S.T.
New York City
(From Luke)

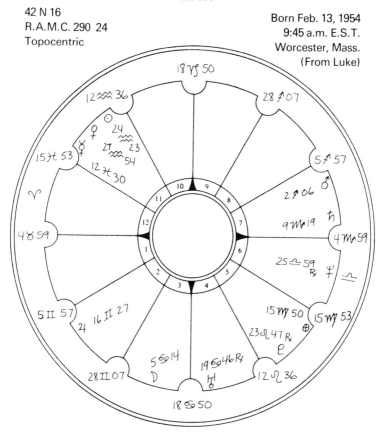

MARY

42 N 16
R.A.M.C. 290 24
Topocentric

Born Feb. 13, 1954
9:45 a.m. E.S.T.
Worcester, Mass.
(From Luke)

MARTHA

42° 16
R.A.M.C. 144 45
Topocentric

Born Oct. 22, 1952
7:22 a.m. E.S.T.
Worcester, Mass.
(From Luke)

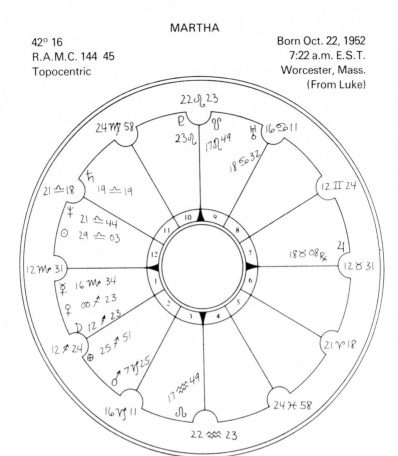

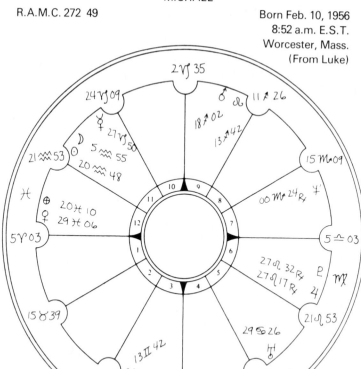

MICHAEL

R.A.M.C. 272 49

Born Feb. 10, 1956
8:52 a.m. E.S.T.
Worcester, Mass.
(From Luke)

She realized that there is at present great interest by everyone in nutrition, and thinks perhaps she would like to be a nutritionist in some distant country. At the moment, Chiron, the newly discovered planet, if planet it be, is transiting her Ascendant, bringing the thought of healing, said to be an attribute of Chiron, into her consciousness. She has been accepted by the Peace Corps and given an assignment teaching nutrition in Nepal.

The contact between Michael's Uranus and his father's Fortuna may have given him his lucky streak. He, too, is a traveller. His mother's Neptune in contact with his Fortuna may be the clue to his restlessness.

> The Road goes ever on and on
> Down from the door where it began
> Now far ahead the Road has gone
> And I must follow if I can,
> Pursuing it with weary feet...

He had crossed the desert by Landrover to Africa and seen the great game herds. He has wandered through the bazaars of Istanbul and sailed among the islands of Greece. He has worked at the marine research center in Panama, and trekked into the interior to visit the primitive Indians. He has flown to Columbia, and made his way by bus to Ecuador where he and a friend tried to climb Chimborao, but failed, being quite unprepared for the conditions they found. He has counted birds for the Fish and Wildlife Service in Alaska, and climbed mountains there. He has taken the overland route by bus and train to Nepal, through Kabul and the Himalayas, and trekked to the base of Everest.

Settle down? Of course not—Neptune drives him ever onward.

There is great interest among astrologers in the hereditary transmission of traits from parents to children, and this may be another way of studying the problem.

Zodiacal contacts are also important. For example, there is a close conjunction between the Uranus-Moon-fifth cusp of the father of this family to the seventh cusp of the mother. This might signify the non-conformist nature of the children, for the tendency has been particularly strong in this family. The mother has Uranus opposed by Saturn, and she has felt the limitations of money and convention. She loves to travel. As soon as she can get enough money for the fare, she is off, and never mind that she has to sleep in a Youth Hostel instead of the Ritz. Naturally she encourages her wandering son and daughter in their perennial junkets around the world.

The father, who has sacrificed his own wants and needs to finance them, has a close conjunction between his Moon and the Sun of Michael, and a wide conjunction with the Sun of Mary. There are many midpoint contacts between the three children and their parents, which I will not go into. One is the conjunction of Mary's Fortuna with the Sun-Moon midpoint of her father, an important emotional tie.

As John Addey has pointed out in his work on harmonics, in all families there is a certain family tradition which runs through several generations of a family and comes out strongly in some members. The O.A. and O.D. contacts may be important, and Fortuna may be a clue. This is a field for astrologers to investigate. We will have to wait for computers to do it, for it has taken me many weary hours to calculate the charts for this one family.

The Use Of Ascensional Directions In Rectification

Anyone who is still with me may wonder why I am so sure about the exact rectification of the charts of the family. There is another use for ascensional directions. The Argentine group claims that any chart can be rectified by taking events which have been exactly timed to the second (a very difficult thing to do in practice), and calculating the charts of these events. There is always, they claim, an exact contact between the natal chart and the chart of the event.

An opportunity to test my rectification was the flight to Europe of Mary and her mother. My reasoning was as follows. If the chart of the father was accurate, Mary's chart and his must have an exact contact, and therefore Mary's chart could be set up accurately by taking the nearest exact contact to the time of birth given by the hospital. The time of the takeoff to Europe could then be compared with the chart of Mary. There must be an ascensional direction which fitted the symbolism of a journey, and the flight chart might have to be altered slightly, since sometimes flights do not leave exactly when they are supposed to.

There was such an ascensional direction. The journey began at Kennedy Airport on February 2, 1976, at 9 p.m. The significant direction was Mary's Jupiter to the transiting Uranus at the time of the flight.

This was astrologically appropriate. The purpose of the journey was to study Chinese in Taiwan. This brings in the archetypes of Jupiter and Uranus without a doubt. The chart of the flight had to be altered only slightly. For once, take off was very close to the scheduled time.

I had approximated the chart of the mother by transits, and now had to find the exact time when an ascensional direction would be exact with an astrologically appropriate one in the chart of the flight.

It turned out that natal Uranus was in ascensional contact with the flight Jupiter. This was the first journey for several years, and she was very excited about it. The symbolism was appropriate. On the return journey, Jupiter was in exact ascensional contact with her natal Moon. She was coming home. The archetypes of astrology are made very clear by ascensional directions.

It is not difficult, once three charts are known to be accurate, to find ascensional directions which fit all three and the two which are unknown. It is like a jigsaw puzzle---only one piece will fit.

The calculations are as follows:

Kennedy Airport 40° 43' N
R.A.M.C. flight 87° 09' or 447° 09'
R.A.M.C. of Mary 290° 24'
By subtraction 156° 45' which is transposition arc
Arc plus Jupiter 64° 11' equals 220° 56'
Transiting Uranus 220° 56'
R.A.M.C. flight 87° 09'
R.A.M.C. mother 36°
Arc 51° 09' plus natal Uranus 331° 19' equals 22° 28'
Transiting Jupiter 22° 28'

We now have an exact R.A.M.C. for the mother. Previously, I had thought it was 37° 20'.

On the following page, there is the chart of an event. Three people were involved.

The importance of Mars in road accidents has been shown by Dr. C. Kuypers, who published a study in *The Astrological Journal* Vol. XX No. 4, Autumn 1978.

In this case, transiting Mars in the fifth house is the partner of a natal planet in an ascensional direction of each of the three people involved.

If #1 is correct, which I believe it to be, then #2 is seven minutes of arc or twenty-eight seconds of time in error. Likewise, #3 is one minute of arc or four seconds of time in error.

The event was a car crash. My car was totalled on a ski trip when a large truck was driven out of a side road directly in front of it. Fortunately, no one was hurt.

#1 was reading a book. Note that natal Mercury is the ruler of her third house, that of short journeys. She had no idea what was happening until the car crashed. The ascension direction was between Mars and her Mercury.

#2 was watching the road and saw what was about to happen. She was very frightened and certain that she would be killed. The A.D. was an opposition between her Neptune and Mars.

#3 was driving my car. He thought that the car, which I had lent to him (note his eleventh house Saturn, the house of friends) would be totalled and everyone killed, and felt responsible, although it was not his fault. His A.D. was between Mars and his Saturn.

The archetypes fit perfectly. It is possible to rectify a chart with several timed events.

A month later, #1, my youngest daughter, won a box of chocolates on a radio show on St. Valentine's Day. I looked at the clock when the announcer said, "You've won!" The chart

CAR CRASH

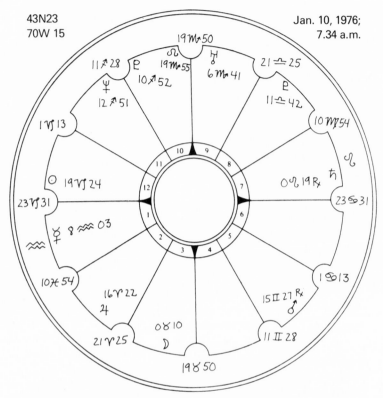

43N23
70W 15

Jan. 10, 1976;
7.34 a.m.

Three people were involved.

R.A.M.C. EVENT 227° 23'   O.D. Mars 85 30

R.A.M.C. # 1 7° 23'

Subtract, arc of transposition is 220°.

Add to Mercury of # 1 at 45° 30'.

45 30 plus 220 equals 265° 30'.

R.A.M.C. # 2 1° 08'

Subtract 1.08 from 227° 23', which equals 226° 15', the arc of transposition.

Add to Neptune of # 2 at 219° 08', which equals 445° 23' or 85° 23'.

R.A.M.C. # 3 194° 08'.

Subtract from R.A.M.C. 227° 23', giving arc of transpostion 33° 15'.

Add to Saturn of # 3 at 232° 14', which equals 265° 29'.

The importance of Mars in road accidents has been shown by Dr. C. Kuypers, who published a study in *The Astrological Journal* Vol. XX No 4, Autumn 1978.

showed Jupiter in exact ascensional conjunction with her natal Venus.

I have set up a great many charts of ascensional directions. My son-in-law had his chart rectified by his first meeting with me. Transiting Pluto was in the first house, opposite my Sun by O.A.-O.D. contact. His Mars was opposition transiting Mercury, my Sun ruler, at the same time, and Mars is his Sun ruler. The rectified time was very close to the time given by his mother and was confirmed by the birth of a son to him and my daughter.

I rectified the chart of one of my sons by setting up the charts of a telephone call he made from Lima, Peru, which was timed electronically by the telephone company, and another telephone call from New Mexico. There were so many possible ascensional directions between his chart and mine that I did not know which was the correct one, and comparison with the charts of the two telephone calls gave me the answer.

In *The Progressed Horoscope*, Alan Leo mentions that if a planet is half way through a house, it is in 'mundane conjunction' with a transiting planet half way through the same house. The idea of ascensional directions is therefore not entirely new. However, it seems that no one worked them out three dimensionally until the Argentine group did so and found that the contact was exact.

It seemed very unlikely that astrologers who are outside the mainstream of astrological practice should come up with such startling and original findings. The Topocentric System was described in a recent review of Wendell Polich's book as the astrological discovery of the century. Yet perhaps it was necessary to be isolated from the mainstreams of Europe and the U.S.A. to develop a concept which originated from the classical work on primary directions by the German astrologers who worked before Hitler. Professor Polich has his roots in Europe, and Tony Nelson Page was an Englishman. It is very sad that his life burned out at an early age, and Wendell Polich has to rely on translations from the Spanish for his work to be put

before the astrological public. Fortunately, I read Spanish
and have written to him about many points which I could not
understand. The Topocentric System will come into its own
one day.

The Prenatal Epoch

God geometrizes.

There is a very old method of rectifying a chart. It is called the Tritune of Hermes, and states:

Every birth has a prenatal epoch, when the Moon at birth or its opposite position is the Ascendant at epoch, and the Ascendant at epoch or its opposite position is the Moon at birth.

Charles Jayne, who has probably worked with the Epoch more than anyone else in the U.S.A., has said that this is only approximately true. If he is right, the Epoch is of no use in rectification.

However, Alexander Markin in England has studied the Epoch and finds that there is a slight modification of its rules. The Vertex may take the place of the Ascendant. This may explain Jayne's findings.

The Epoch is not the chart of conception, as was thought. I have accurate conception times of several births, none corresponding to the Epoch. It appears to be the time of implantation of the ovum, or when ovum and sperm meet. It may be the moment of the entrance of the soul.

There are two difficulties in calculating the Epoch. One is that the movement of the Moon is irregular, and it is not easy to calculate accurately. One must use a special formula with second corrections, or have it calculated by a computer. It moves about one minute of arc in two minutes of time, and this can make a difference of almost a degree on the Ascendant.

The second difficulty is almost insurmountable. One has to know the whereabouts of the mother at the time of the Epoch!

I believe that the tradition is true. If the birth chart is accurate, a prenatal epoch can be found at the time when the ovum is implanted and begins to grow.

I present here, for the first time in astrological history (as far as I know), three charts, those of conception, epoch, and birth. They are of my own child.

I was living in New Hampshire at the time and visiting relations in England. The first chart, that of conception, is drawn for Snainton, just six miles from Scarborough in Yorkshire. I was there for about five days.

The epoch occured in Leyburn a week later.

She was born in New Hampshire. Had I not known these facts, it would have been quite impossible to have calculated the charts.

It is a Vertex epoch. These are rare, and seem to mark out those who have a message for the world, or a task to perform. Alexander Markin wrote, "These seem to be people who are exceptional. They stand apart from their contemporaries as though from another planet (which, for all one knows, they might be)."

I rectified the natal chart by the Topocentric system, both by primary directions and by comparison with the known O.A./O.D. points of both parents. She was born at home, rather precipitously, and delivered by her father and a neighbor. Even though I had asked for the first breath to be noted, the astrological time of birth was five minutes earlier than the time recorded. Perhaps it was because she was born in a caul and the membranes had to be cut to extricate her.

I sent the computer service of Neil Michelson the R.A.M.C. calculated for an ascendant opposite the birth Moon. It seemed to be the only possible time for the Epoch, knowing the time of conception. The chart I received showed the Moon conjunct the natal Vertex, and it was close, although not exact to the minute. Her father's Epoch chart exactly confirms his birth chart and mine too. The cause of this is not clear to me. She was born with the Moon near the horizon, when parallax is maximum, and the Moon might need to be corrected for parallax.

The M.Do's of all six charts are shown in the table.

As explained, the M.Do's measure the true distance to the meridian. Planets with equal M.Do's are in ascensional conjunction. The M.Do is equal to 90 multiplied by the fraction M.D./S.A. The S.A. must be larger than the M.D.

The M.D. (meridian distance) is measured in degrees of right ascension from the meridian, and the R.A. of each planet must be calculated.

The R.A.M.C. of each chart heads the column.

	FATHER		MOTHER		EPOCH		BIRTH		CONCEP-TION		DEATH	
RAMC	259	38	233	54	101	19	277	34	278	16	315	46
Sun	12	13	67	39	27	42	77	41	47	06	17	18
Moon	72	49	45	47	88	45	83	01	38	24	59	46
Mercury	37	47	45	47	55	37	89	26	67	56	23	12
Venus	54	47	68	53	64	44	87	07	70	29	5	35
Mars	70	58	28	04	13	19	66	44	21	10	34	09
Jupiter	83	36	21	12	82	19	79	05	89	26	33	23
Saturn	79	36	68	53	75	50	88	37	84	47	40	23
Uranus	89	26	89	26	1	04	5	13	7	09	61	23
Neptune	75	06	76	08	78	28	83	55	89	08	89	26
Pluto	27	26	42	42	30	50	64	28	77	34	64	38
Fortuna	33	47	15	06	33	11	75	59	85	52	4	28
Node	58	34	68	29	55	01	60		72	56	85	

Mercury in the birth chart and Jupiter in the conception chart have exactly the same M.Do as Neptune in the death chart. The Epoch chart has no ascensional contact, and probably does not correspond to a physical event, or is not properly calculated.

Although the mathematics are difficult to understand, the Topocentric system has solved the problem of house cusps in the Polar Zone. As the Topocentric houses divide the ecliptic by the passage of Time as well as by Space, the temporal horizon can produce house cusps. It happens that the horizon of a place and the plane of the Prime Vertical of its co-latitude coincide exactly. The topocentric solution is to work with the Prime Vertical of the co-latitude, and where the plane of the Prime Vertical cuts the Ecliptic, the true Ascendant is found.

For those like me, who were born near the Equator and want to find the Vertex, there is a simple formula in Polich's book, *The Topocentric System.* There is also a Table of Houses for Polar regions.

I sought in vain for a prenatal Epoch for my chart, and only when I used the Polar Tables to find my true Veretex did I solve the problem, for I too have a Vertex Epoch and it confirms my rectified birth chart exactly.

BRONWYN

Conception Chart

54N 17 0W 24

10:57 p.m. summer time
Aug. 1, 1951
Snainton, Yorks

R.A.M.C. 278 16

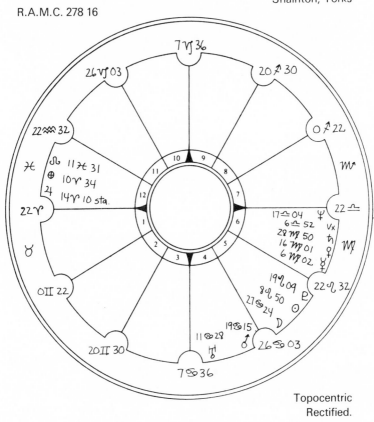

Topocentric
Rectified.

Epoch chart

54N 18
1W 50

R.A.M.C. 101 19

9:52. 09 a.m.
G.M.T.
Aug. 7, 1951.
Leyburn, Yorks

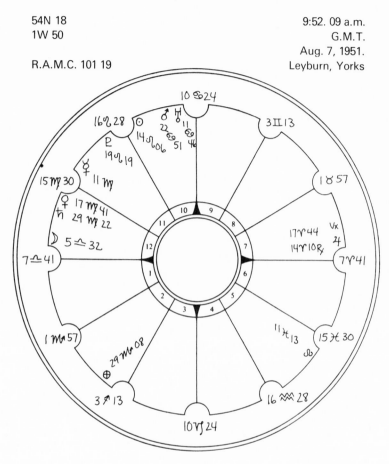

Topocentric.

BRONWYN

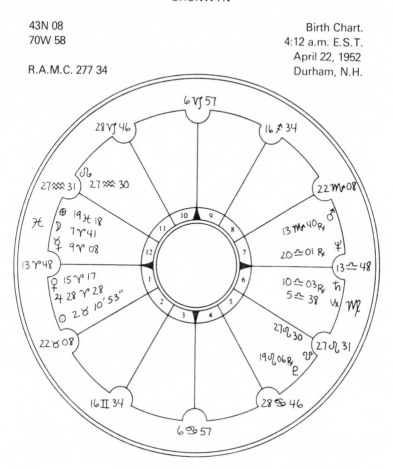

43N 08
70W 58

R.A.M.C. 277 34

Birth Chart.
4:12 a.m. E.S.T.
April 22, 1952
Durham, N.H.

6 ♑ 57

28 ♑ 46   16 ♐ 34

27 ♒ 31   ☋ 27 ♒ 30   22 ♏ 08

♃   ⊕ 19 ♓ 18
☽ 7 ♈ 41   13 ♏ 40 ℞ ♂
☿ 9 ♈ 08   20 ♎ 01 ℞ ♆

13 ♈ 48   13 ♎ 48

10   9
11   8
12   7
1   6
2   5
3   4

♀ 15 ♈ 17   10 ♎ 03 ℞ ♄
♃ 28 ♈ 28   5 ♎ 38   Vx ♍
☉ 28 ♉ 10′53″

22 ♉ 08   27 ♌ 30   27 ♌ 31

19 ♌ 06 ℞ ♇ 28

16 ♊ 34   28 ♋ 46

6 ♋ 57

Topocentric
Rectified

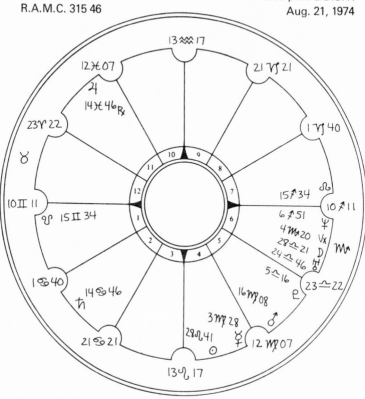

43N 44
70W 16

R.A.M.C. 315 46

Death of Bronwyn
from pulmonary edema.
11:43.50 p.m. E.D.S.T.
Aug. 21, 1974

Topocentric
Rectified

Wherever She May Be

My daughter Bronyn was very beautiful. When she was born, I looked at her chart, with Venus rising and the 7th cusp bracketed between Saturn and Neptune, and I realised that her hold on life would be tenuous. She was destined to die at the age of 22, when Mars by primary direction came to the 7th cusp. It will be seen that Mars is the natal ruler of the 8th house, and afflicts Pluto in the 5th. Karma was involved, and the death chart showed Mars opposition Jupiter, the signature of Victory, in a degree associated with the Rosy Cross. The transiting Sun was with Regulus, the Heart of the Lion, and signified that by her pain and her courage, she had paid her debt. I do not know where she is, but I am certain that she will always be loved, wherever she may be.

Bronwyn was born with multiple heart defects. In effect, she had a two-chambered heart imperfectly divided into four, and a severe pulmonic stenosis.

At one year, she weighed eleven pounds. She was not strong enough to take in enough calories to grow. On her first birthday, she was in an oxygen tent in Boston Children's Hospital. We were told that the outlook was very poor. She was in heart failure. It was only the first of many hospital admissions.

Every age has its sacrificial lambs. Bronwyn, with Aries rising, was to put up a tremendous struggle for life, and to act as an experimental object on which doctors could learn the skills they needed to save the lives of other children with congenital heart disease. She was destined to be one of the pioneers of the new age of heart surgery, and to suffer greatly in the process.

Even cardiac catheterisation, now so routine, had not been fully developed at that time. Bronwyn had one of the first to be done, and her heart arrested at the first attempt, when the catheter reached her heart after being threaded through the long blood vessel from her groin. The procedure had to be repeated when she was four, and she remembered for the rest of her life being tied down on the table, and the novocaine, which soon wore off, being injected around the vein. The report said laconically, "Owing to the uncooperative behavior of the child, the study was unsatisfactory." It is not an easy study to carry out on a child. It caused so much irregularity of the heart that we were forced to leave her in the hospital for two weeks, and when a nurse found her crying after we left, she slapped her and called her a little coward. This was the first of many painful procedures. We were told by her cardiologist that the operation would either kill her, or make her normal."

Heart surgery had begun, but was still in its infancy, and the techniques had not yet been perfected when she finally came to the stage when she could live no longer without it. Her failing heart muscle could not pump the blood through the narrow pulmonary artery to her lungs, and she went into severe congestive heart failure.

It was July 24, 1962. Bronwyn was ten. The fifth floor of Boston Children's Hospital was full of doomed children with congenital heart disease. There were four others with defects as serious as her's.

There was great tension on the ward. Results lately had been poor. The mortality approached 50%. The ritual bath and shampoo with phisohex on the night before surgery was like some primitive pre-sacrificial rite.

The five severe cases were all operated upon in a five day period. Lisa, aged four, had tricuspid atresia, and Bronwyn had talked to her and cheered her, so she went happily into surgery. She never came out. "We could not stop the bleeding," the house officer told me.

Jeff was the second case, and he had been chasing all over the ward, pushing trolleys and playing ball in the corridors. He was nine, and had Tetralogy of Fallot, which had to have an anatomical repair. As he had already had a palliative procedure, he looked very healthy, but he went into congestive heart failure when the team took him off the heart-lung pump, and he too did not return from surgery.

John, a physician's grandson, who was fifteen, died of 'pump lung' three days after his repair. Lucy was returned to the ward without her operation, as they found no developed pulmonary artery when they opened her chest. It was a bad week, and one of the house officers resigned and went into another branch of surgery. Of the five cases, only Bronwyn was operated on and survived.

It is very painful to breathe when the sternum has been split to open the chest. The surgery had lasted for six hours, and patches had been sewn into the heart wall to separate the chambers and into the pulmonary artery to enlarge it. The pump room, where all the patients who had survived their surgery were held for five days, was kept cold to lower the metabolic rate and reduce the demands on the heart. Each bed had a respirator beside it, and the patients were made to inflate their chests to the full capacity several times every hour, to prevent collapsed lungs. There were bright lights, monitors, and a house officer always on the floor in case of an emergency. On the fifth day, we received chilling news. A needle had been left inside her chest cavity, and they wanted to operate again to remove it.

The second operation lasted six hours, and opened up two new incisions across her chest, as well as the original one in the midline. The needle was never found.

Bronwyn became breathless, and pneumonia set in. She was given an overdose of digitalis, and the error was barely caught in time. Her lung collapsed. She had antibiotic injections every four hours, and her weight dropped alarmingly. Finally we took her home against medical advice, because we thought she would die of starvation.

Her condition improved, but her heart after all did not

repair. The tricuspid valve became more and more incompetant. She had chronic right-sided congestive heart failure, and the only hope appeared to be to have a new valve put in.

We would not return to Boston, but one of the best surgeons in the world operated at the Mayo Clinic hospital, and in November 1968, I flew with her to Rochester, having come to the end of the line. She was so swollen from congestive failure that they did not repeat the cardiac catheterisation, but operated on her for a valve replacement at once.

Dr. Magoon's patients had a green shamrock on their doors. We found her shamrock in her jewelry box six years later, among her most valuable possessions.

The valve was repaired. No one knew how long artificial valves would last and it seemed better to preserve her own.

Brownyn graduated from high school with her class, after a year spent with a home tutor. She joined a troup of actors who were playing summer stock on the Maine coast. Later that year, she went to London and worked with La Mama, an experimental theater group. She studied yoga, body dynamics, and theatrical techniques. It was obvious that she was going to be a very good actress, and this was the happiest time in her life. Those with a strong emphasis on Fire in their charts are often gifted in the arts. After acting as stage manager for a famous English director, she came home and entered college as a theater major.

Bronwyn did not live very long, but she did make a name for herself. At Brandeis, she was considered to be one of the most talented students they had ever had. Her last performance, which was almost a solo in a one act play, was given outstanding praise, and a brilliant future seemed to lie ahead.

Bacterial endocarditis is a serious complication of heart disease. The heart valves become infected, and it is difficult to cure. One got the impression that Bronwyn was driving herself to the limit. She was burning herself out, determined not to let any mere problem of a weak body stop her. In November 1963, she was hospitalized with streptococcal endocarditis, and the treatment for it introduced a new infection into her bloodstream. Her blood began to break down, a rather mysterious rare process known as hemolytic anemia. She returned home in March 1974, and in desperation, we flew once more to the Mayo Clinic.

The valve replacement was made, but too late. She had driven herself to the brink. "I say to my body, just one more step," she wrote, "but Death will not be cheated."

It was very hot on August 21, 1974. It was difficult to breathe, and even a fan to stir the air did not help. At 11:20 P.M. A friend who was staying to look after her woke us and said that Bronwyn was short of breath. "You seem to be breathing, Bron," I said, and she replied, "My diaphragm moves, but no air seems to get in." "Do you want to go to the hospital?" I asked her. "They will give you oxygen, but I must put some pyjamas on you." "It will be too late," she murmured, and twenty minutes later, in the car, she stopped breathing.

I could almost see the unseen Presences who thronged around us to welcome her home.

The Phoenix

Phoenix rises, flies to the Sun, destroyed in golden flames,
Rebirth. Reborn.
The hawk flies, the falcon cries, the dove dies.
We are the deeds of man, sung and unsung,
Like the phoenix, fly us to the Sun.
Rebirth. Reborn.
What is done, is done.

Bronwyn Millard (1952-1974)

The birth chart is a record of the past successes and failures of the Soul.

The death chart also is chosen by the Soul. It represents the fruits of life.

All the talents that have been given to the Soul are perfected and at the hour of death, they are returned to the Cosmos. Turning points in life are shown by the positions of the planets at death.

For example, Venus is the planet of Love. At the time of Bronwyn's first operation, Saturn stood in 8 Aquarius; and at death, Venus marked the point where she had learned love on the fifth floor of the cardiac ward at Boston Children's Hospital.

In April 1953, at the time she lay in an oxygen tent on her first birthday, the Soul must have made up its mind to stay when it could have gone. Saturn then was in 24 Libra and Uranus in 14 Cancer. These points were marked at death, when Uranus was in 24 Libra and Saturn in 14 Cancer.

An astrologer wrote her epitaph as follows:

"It is outstanding that Bron passed away with the Sun with Regulus-Cor Leonis, the Heart of the Lions—one of the noblest Stars in the Heavens. She, whose physical body was so disordered, has won a heart, in every sense. At death, we go in the Direction of the Sun. She made a gift of great courage and will, which others can draw upon for strength. She knows her work is accomplished, and not just for herself, but for others, too. She is sure to return with some great mission."

The world will be waiting.

Glossary

Apnea. The cessation of respiration.

Bilirubin Lights. Fluorescent lights of a certain wavelength which breaks down the bilirubin of the blood to colorless and presumably harmless compounds. A blood level in a newborn of over 15 mg percent of bilirubin can cause brain damage.

Blood Pressure. Normally, around 120/80. Very low or absent blood pressure indicates shock or heart failure. Extremely high blood pressure can cause hemorrhage into the brain (a stroke or shock) or failure of the pumping action of the heart.

Bone Age. X rays of the wrist, elbow and other bones are used to estimate the chronological age. In thyroid failure, a child will have a bone age well below its actual age, and this is used as a test.

Cirrhosis of the Liver. The liver cells are damaged and shrunken, and there is an excess of the normal fibrous tissue in which they lie.

CT Scan. A technique which utilizes whole body scanning in three dimensions-tomography—linked to a computer—hence computerized axial tomography. It is used in cases of suspected brain injury or disease to diagnose intracranial hemorrhage, tumor and enlargement of the ventricles.

Colostomy. A surgical operation which brings the bowel out on to the abdominal wall, thus by-passing the rectum.

Encephalopathy. Inflammation of the brain, associated with virus infection or metabolic disease.

D.E.S. daughters. The daughters of the women who were given diethyl stilbestrol during pregnancy in an effort to prevent miscarriage. They are known to be at risk of developing carcinoma of the vagina.

Dopamine. Given by intravenous infusion to keep up the blood pressure

Fibroids. Fibrous growths of the uterine wall which are non-malignant but cause excessive bleeding and are thought to be due to hormone imbalance.

Foramem Magnum. The hole in the base of the skull through which pass important bloodvessels as well as the spinal cord. If the spinal cord is compressed by being forced down into the foramen magnum, the patient is said to "cone" his brain, and death results.

Gamma Globulin. The antibodies found in the blood, manufactured by certain lymphocytes, and neccessary to combat infection. A patient with deficient antibody production will die, unless given gamma globulin.

Glycogen. The carbohydrate form in which the liver stores its precursor of blood glucose.

Hecate. Goddess of witches, see The White Goddess by Robert Graves.

Hyaline Membrane disease. A common cause of death in premature babies, named from the hyaline membrane which surrounds the lungs. The main defect is now known to be a lack of surfactant, which causes the lungs to open up for aeration easily.

I.G.A. One part of the gamma globulins, which are called gamma A, or I.G.A. gamma G and gamma E.

Hypoglycemia. Low blood sugar.

Levine Tube. A rubber tube which is placed in the stomach in an unconscious patient to drain it.

Malignant Melanoma. A very unpredictable and usually fatal form of cancer affecting the melanin-producing cells of the skin or retina. Melanin is said to be controlled by the hormone of the pineal gland.

Optic Chiasma. The nerve connection between the eye and the brain.

Otitis Media. Middle ear disease, usually caused by bacterial infection.

Renal Shutdown. The kidneys fail to function, and no urine is formed.

Surfactant. A substance which is formed in the lungs during the last few weeks of pregnancy, and which helps them expand.

Temporal Lobe Seizures—those originating from the temporal lobe of the brain, which, since it does not supply impulses to muscles, does not cause the characteristic movements of other seizures but manifest as behavior changes.

Thymus. A gland prominent in early childhood which is an organ of immunity and of growth.

Vasopressor. A drug causing an increase in blood pressure.

Wilson's Disease. A hereditary dominant disorder of copper metabolism, in which the liver becomes progressively more damaged by deposits in it of copper.

Bibliographical References

Chapter 2

Charles E.O. Carter. *An Encyclopedia of Psychological Astrology.* Theosophical Publishing House.

Margot Mason. *The Power of your Thoughts.* ASTROLOGY NOW. Vol. 1, No. 3.

Margaret Millard. *Timing in Medical Astrology.* ASTROLOGY NOW. Vol. 1, No. 7. October 1975.

Dennis Elwell. *Tune In To The Cosmos.* AMERICAN ASTROLOGY. Jan. 1970.

Dennis Elwell. *Try Equal Houses.* AMERICAN ASTROLOGY. Nov. 1967.

Robert Hand. *A New Approach to Transits.* THE COSMOCOLOGY BULLETIN. No. 4. June 1976. Association for Research in Cosmocology.

Chapter 3

Chester Kemp. *A Simple Theory and Its Application.* SPICA, Vol. 8. Oct. 1978.

R.C. Firebrace. *Astrology, Moray Series No. 4.* TERTIARY DIRECTIONS.

Chapter 4

Charles E.O. Carter. *An Encyclopedia of Psychological Astrology.* Theosophical Publishing House.

Zipporah Pottenger Dobyns. *The Asteroid Ephemeris.* T.I.A. Publications.

Margaret Millard. ASTROLOGY NOW. Vol. 1, No. 7. October 1975.

Dennis Elwell. *Tune In to the Cosmos.* AMERICAN ASTROLOGY. Nov. 1967.

Dennis Elwell. *Try Equal Houses.* AMERICAN ASTROLOGY. Nov. 1967.

Robert Hand. *A New Approach to Transits.* THE COSMO-COLOGY BULLETIN. No. 4. June 1976. Assoc. for Research in Cosmocology.

Chester Kemp. *A Simple Theory and Its Application.* SPICA, Vol. 8. Oct. 1968.

R.C. Firebrace. *Astrology, Moray Series No. 4.*

Chapter 5

J.W. Shaffer and C.W. Schmidt. ARCHIVE OF GENERAL PSYCHIATRY, No. 35. Jan. 1977.

Garth Allen. AMERICAN ASTROLOGY, No. 31. Nov. 1963.

Michael Munkasey. THE MERCURY HOUR, No. 13. April 1977.

Chapter 6

John Addey. *Harmonics in Astrology.* Cambridge Circle Ltd., 1976.

Chapter 12

Garth Allen. *Murder Will Out.* AMERICAN ASTROLOGY. Feb. 1957.

Reinhold Ebertin. *The Combination of Stellar Influences.*

Chapter 14

Dennis Elwell. *An Astrologer Looks at Death.* AMERICAN ASTROLOGY DIGEST, Vol. 22. 1977.

Charles E.O. Carter. *Infant Mortality: Some Principles of Horoscopic Delineation.* W. Foulsham and Co.

Chapter 16

Frida G. Surawicz. *Women, Cancer and Emotions.* Journal American Women's Assoc., 1977.

British Medical Journal. *Is Cancer Irreversible?* (Editorial). No. 2, 1978.

F.M. Burnet. *Immunological Surveillance.* Pergamon Press. Oxford; 1970.

L. Le Shan. *Psychological Factors in the Development of Malignant Disease.* Journal National Cancer Institute, 1959.

Robert Hand. *Planets in Transit.* Para Research Inc., 1976.

Alan Houghton, et al. *Increased Incidence of Malignant Melanoma after Peaks of Sunspot Activity.* LANCET, 1978.

J. Eddy. *Sunspot Activity.* SCIENCE, 1976.

J.N. Bhasin. *Medical Astrology: A Rational Approach.* Sagar Publications, New Delhi.

Constance Holden. *Cancer and the Mind: How Are They Connected?* SCIENCE, Vol. 200. June 1978.

Peggy Roggenbach. *The Good News About Cancer.* NEW AGE JOURNAL. May 1978.

Chapter 24

Dr W.D. Davidson. *Your Life Span.* AMERICAN ASTROLOGY DIGEST, Vol. 19., 1974.

Chapter 26

Robert Carl Jansky. *Astrology Nutrition and Health.* Para Research Inc., 1977.

Chapter 32

Wendell Polich. *The Topocentric System.* Editorial Regulus, Buenos Aires, 1975.

A.P. Nelson Page. *Spica:* Vol. 4 No. 2, Vol. 4 No. 3, Vol. 4 No. 4, Vol. 5 No. 1, Vol. 5 No. 2.

ASTROLOGY

THE PRENATAL EPOCH. *E.H. Bailey*
Rectification of recorded birth times and the calculation of the time of birth from past events with reference to Epochal Laws. New York, 1974. 239 pp.

THE ZODIAC AND THE SALTS OF SALVATION.
George Washington Carey and *Inez Eudora Perry.*
The Relation of the Mineral Salts of the Body to the Signs of the Zodiac and an esoteric analysis and synthesis of the Zodiacal Signs and their physical-chemical allocations. New York, 1977. 352 pp.

THE ASTROLOGY OF I CHING. *W.K. Chu* and *W.A. Sherrill.*
The greater the understanding one has of the I Ching, the Book of Changes, the more accurate will one's interpretation be of the Astrology of I Ching. Both are based on the same concepts and derivations. Both share in ageless Chinese knowledge and philosophy. New York, 1976. 443 pp.

THE ASTROLOGY OF ANCIENT ISRAEL: "TO RULE BOTH DAY AND NIGHT". *Rabbi Joel C. Dobin.*
Traces the lost line of astrology through the western tradition as far back as the second millenium B.C., describing ancient Israel's understanding and use of astrology as a divine science. New York, 1977. 240 pp.

THE NEW WAITE'S COMPENDIUM OF NATAL ASTROLOGY. *Colin Evans.*
With Ephemeris for 1870 to 1980 and Universal Table of Houses. New York, 1976. 246 pp.

RELATING: AN ASTROLOGICAL GUIDE TO LIVING WITH OTHERS ON A SMALL PLANET. *Liz Greene.*
Dr. Greene uses basic astrological concepts symbolically and practically in a framework of Jungian psychology, to show the ways in which people relate to one another on both conscious and unconscious levels. An original, advanced, information-packed, provocative and well-organized work. New York, 1977. 289 pp.

SATURN: A NEW LOOK AT AN OLD DEVIL. *Liz Greene.*
A major step in the unveiling of the light of reason so long obscured by those who have interpreted Saturn as a "malefic" planet. Tracing the character of this most important planet through sign, house, aspect and synastry, and its role in mythology, Dr. Greene introduces us to Saturn who hides himself in a mask of sorrow which, when removed, reveals the face of the Initiator. New York, 1976. 200 pp. Paper.

PLUTO-NEPTUNE. *Germaine Holley.*
This book on the Pluto-Neptune dual rulership of the sign Pisces goes beyond an analysis of psychological conditioning, opening the gate to a new philosophical perspective. New York, 1975. 160 pp. Paper.

A GUIDE TO QABALISTIC ASTROLOGY. *Horus.*
Drawing heavily on the ideas expounded by Aleister Crowley in *Astrology* and *777,* Horus develops and synthesizes a new system of correspondences. Taking into consideration the more recent discoveries of the outer planets Neptune, Uranus and Pluto, he reassigns the attributions of the planets to the Tree of Life. New York, 1977. Paper.

THE COMPLETE DICTIONARY OF ASTROLOGY. *Alan Leo.*
A handy reference text of all the terms and concepts you will need to understand astrology in its technical and philosophical dimensions. New York, 1978. 203 pp. Paper.

ESOTERIC ASTROLOGY. *Alan Leo.*
This work deals with Natal Astrology in a manner never before attempted by any writer on astrology. Divided into three parts, the first part explains the theoretical aspect of Esoteric Astrology; the second demonstrates the practical side of Esoteric Astrology with many examples; and the third part deals with the subdivisions of the Zodiac. New York, 1978. 293 pp. Paper.

JUPITER. *Alan Leo.*
Jupiter is presented as the Preserver, remarkable for its own symbolism and its relation to other symbols. New York, 1977. 88 pp. Paper.

THE KEY TO YOUR OWN NATIVITY. *Alan Leo.*
A complete and comprehensive analysis of all the elements of the horoscope, giving full descriptions of every position in the nativity. New York, 1978. 303 pp. Paper.

MARS. *Alan Leo.*
The horoscopes of ten famous people used to illustrate the significant part Mars plays in life. New York, 1978. 99 pp. Paper.

THE PROGRESSED HOROSCOPE. *Alan Leo.*
The most comprehensive guide to the system of predicting the future. The methods for drawing up annual forecasts and divining upcoming influences are completely outlined, including detailed and fully delineated aspects. New York, 1978. 353 pp. Paper.

SATURN. *Alan Leo.*
The importance of Saturn in the transmutation of the whole man from the mundane to the spiritual. New York, 1977. Paper.

AN ASTROLOGICAL KEY TO BIBLICAL SYMBOLISM. *Ellen McCaffery.*
The occult wisdom of the Bible interpreted through the medium of astrology. New York, 1975.

THE GNOSTIC CIRCLE. *Patrizia Norelli-Bachelet.*
This book is a synthesis of the Zodiac and the Enneagram which shows the diverse occult forces that pervade life and the cosmic harmony that results when these forces interweave. Includes detailed color charts and information on how an individual can find his or her place in the Divine Mosaic. New York, 1978. 310 pp. Paper.

TRANSCENDENTAL ASTROLOGY. *A.G. Norris.*
The planetary numerals and symbolism and the lessons of the signs delineated to enable an astrologer to link the soul to the astrological chart. New York, 1978. 288 pp.

BEGINNERS GUIDE TO PRACTICAL ASTROLOGY.
An introductory book on astrology containing the essential information necessary to a practical investigation of astrological claims. New York, 1976. 176 pp. Paper.

THE FIXED STARS AND CONSTELLATIONS IN ASTROLOGY.
Contains much of what has been written on this subject since the Middle Ages. New York, 1976. 264 pp.

KARMIC ASTROLOGY VOLUME I: THE MOON'S NODES AND REINCAR-NATION. *Martin Schulman.*
After introductory chapters on *Reincarnation and Karma* and *The Astrology of Reincarnation,* THE MOON'S NODES AND REINCARNATION gives a complete delineation of the nodes by sign and house position; a chapter on aspects to the nodes; sample delineations; and an appendix giving nodal positions from 1850 to 2000A.D. New York, 1976. 132 pp. Paper.

KARMIC ASTROLOGY VOLUME II: RETROGRADES AND REINCARNA-TION. *Martin Schulman.*
One of the most radical and unorthodox interpretations of retrograde planets ever published, this book explains the three vibrational moods in which retrogrades may be expressed. Each planet is discussed thoroughly in all signs and houses with an examination of the esoteric and karmic symbolism involved. New York, 1977. 208 pp. Paper.

KARMIC ASTROLOGY VOLUME III: JOY AND THE PART OF FORTUNE. *Martin Schulman.*
This book covers placement of the Part of Fortune in the twelve signs and houses with example charts and delineations of nativities. Throughout, the Laws of Karma are related to this most mysterious and vital point in the horoscope. New York, 1978. Paper.

KARMIC ASTROLOGY VOLUME IV: THE KARMA OF THE NOW. *Martin Schulman.*
This final volume of the Karmic Astrology Series describes the merging of Astrology with reality as it truly is—based on the understanding that the past and future exist only as a person thinks. New York, 1978. Paper.

A MANUAL OF ASTROLOGY.
Four books in one including the Language of the Heavens, the Reading of a Horoscope, the Measure of Time and Hindu Astrology. New York, 1972. 228 pp. Paper.

ASTROLOGICAL CYCLES AND THE LIFE CRISIS PERIODS. *John Townley.*
This book explains the repeating cycles manifested in man and nature, from full-moon lunacy to social upheaval. Special emphasis on the psychological personality-crisis periods of the individual—when they occur and how people deal with them. New York, 1978. Paper.

THE COMPOSITE CHART. *John Townley.*
This is a new technique in the ancient art of horoscope comparison. New York 1974. Paper.

URANUS: ESOTERIC AND MUNDANE. *John Townley.*
This comprehensive and contemporary discussion of Uranus examines its effec in notable nativities, its influence on sexuality and its importance in the natur of consciousness. New York, 1978. 128 pp. Paper.

THE MOON'S NODES. *G. White.*
The Nodes and their importance in Natal Astrology. New York, 1976. 74 pp Paper.

DICTIONARY OF ASTROLOGY. *James Wilson.*
Arranged in alphabetical order, this book extensively covers subjects such a horary astrology, directions, progressions, ingresses, etc. New York, 1978. 40 pp.

ASTROLOGY AND REINCARNATION VOLUME I: RETROGRADE PLANET AND REINCARNATION. *Donal Yott.*
Provides a thorough explanation of the retrograde condition of each plane through the twelve houses, including analysis of retrogrades in aspect. Ne York, 1977. Paper.

ASTROLOGY AND REINCARNATION VOLUME II: INTERCEPTED SIGN AND REINCARNATION. *Donald Yott.*
Examines each interception and its opposite as they appear through the house of the zodiac, showing how we may transmute our past weaknesses into preser strengths in order to perfect ourselves as human beings. New York, 1977. 6 pp. Paper.